D1356472

▶ **Policing the Inner City in France, Britain, and the US**

DOI: 10.1057/9781137428004.0001

Europe in Crisis

Series Editor: **Martin Schain**

The current crisis in Europe has often been depicted as an economic/currency crisis that poses a danger for European economic unity and its common currency, the Euro. Monetary union, it has been argued, has outrun fiscal union, depriving the EU of an important means of dealing with the pressures on the currency. It has also been understood as a crisis of governance, of institutions with the decision-making capacity to deal with the crisis. Finally, the impact of the economic emergency has altered the political landscape in different EU countries in different ways.

The crisis appears to be creating changes that will endure, but cannot yet be predicted entirely. This series fills an important gap in scholarship by supporting a level of analysis that is more thoughtful than the periodic media coverage and less complicated than much of the deep theoretical analysis. These books are timely and concise with the promise of a long lifetime of relevancy.

Titles Include:

Irwin Wall
FRANCE VOTES
The Election of François Hollande

Sophie Body-Gendrot and Catherine Wihtol de Wenden
POLICING THE INNER CITY IN FRANCE, BRITAIN, AND THE US

DOI: 10.1057/9781137428004.0001

palgrave▸pivot

Policing the Inner City in France, Britain, and the US

▸ Sophie Body-Gendrot
University of the Sorbonne, Paris, France

and

Catherine Wihtol de Wenden
Director of Studies, National Center for Scientific Research

palgrave
macmillan

DOI: 10.1057/9781137428004.0001

POLICING THE INNER CITY IN FRANCE, BRITAIN, AND THE US
Copyright © Sophie Body-Gendrot and Catherine Wihtol de Wenden, 2014.

First published in 2014 by
PALGRAVE MACMILLAN®
in the United States—a division of St. Martin's Press LLC,
175 Fifth Avenue, New York, NY 10010.

Where this book is distributed in the UK, Europe and the rest of the world,
this is by Palgrave Macmillan, a division of Macmillan Publishers Limited,
registered in England, company number 785998, of Houndmills, Basingstoke,
Hampshire RG21 6XS.

Palgrave Macmillan is the global academic imprint of the above companies
and has companies and representatives throughout the world.

Palgrave® and Macmillan® are registered trademarks in the United States,
the United Kingdom, Europe and other countries.

ISBN: 978-1-137-42801-1 EPUB
ISBN: 978-1-137-42800-4 PDF
ISBN: 978-1-137-42799-1 Hardback

Library of Congress Cataloging-in-Publication Data is available from
the Library of Congress.

A catalogue record of the book is available from the British Library.

First edition: 2014

www.palgrave.com/pivot

DOI: 10.1057/9781137428004

Special thanks to
Anne-Marie SIMONNOT, IEP Rennes, internship at CERI,
Summer 2013
Julien Gillaizeau, IEP Paris, internship at CERI,
Summer 2013
Parjest Prophyl, NYU Paris, graduate student,
June 2014

DOI: 10.1057/9781137428004.0001

Contents

DOI: 10.1057/9781137428004.0001

Series Editor's Foreword

This book has been "in development" for almost ten years. It began as a research project that was undertaken with the cooperation of the French Ministry of Social Affairs, a project that dealt only with the French police during the years before the riots of young people in the suburbs (the equivalent of the inner city in the US) in 2005. When the French study was first published, the publisher was so enthusiastic, he advertised it as a book "that every minister of the interior must read." Evidently, the minister of the interior at the time, Nicolas Sarkozy, took this advice to heart, and then prevented the authorization of a distribution code, which in turn prevented the book's distribution to bookstores. At the same time, the publisher of the French study went bankrupt.

Nevertheless, the authors of this study were determined to find a way to distribute their results to a wide public, interested in the work of the police. In this book they have updated their work, and re-examined their results in a comparative context. The result of this courageous determination is one of the few comparative studies of how the police deal with urban unrest in three countries in which cycles of riots have punctuated urban life for more than 40 years. This is a critical analysis, based on both original research and analysis of a massive literature on urban unrest.

The authors are two of the most prominent scholars in France. Sophie Body-Gendrot has written on cities and urban unrest for more than 30 years. She is also one of the leading Americanists in France, and has worked in both Britain and the US. Catherine de Wenden is a leading scholar who pioneered the study of the politics of immigration in France. Together, they not only brought a unique perspective to the understanding of how the police deal with urban unrest, but also how they deal with issues of immigration and race in three countries. This book is the culmination of a research project that has endured far longer than either author thought it would, but that has taken on new life in a comparative context.

Martin A. Schain
Professor of Politics, New York University
Series Editor

DOI: 10.1057/9781137428004.0002

1

Introduction

Abstract: *Most Western cities experience difficult encounters between the police and marginalized youths in the inner cities. Some of them may lead to unrest which is disturbing for the localities where they occur. A cross-national comparison is treacherous because countries are not of the same size, the institutions respect common law or civil law, the state intervenes more or less in social processes, anti-discrimination policies have diverse degrees of legitimacy, rebellious youths have different profiles and so do policemen in the three observed countries. The complexity of such comparisons prevents simplistic universalism and ethnocentrism. The aim of such research is to start a debate on very complex issues.*

Body-Gendrot, Sophie and Catherine Wihtol de Wenden. *Policing the Inner City in France, Britain, and the US.* New York: Palgrave Macmillan, 2014. DOI: 10.1057/9781137428004.0003.

The relationship between police, young residents, and minorities from European marginalized inner cities has, for a long time, been a culture of denial, as if those living there would be illegitimate or second- class citizens because they are poor, young, and of foreign origin, permanently questioning the status of their citizenship. In these areas, the interaction between police and young people are difficult for most inhabitants of inner cities, requiring more protection, while demanding the end of police abuse. The problem is typical in various ways of many cities in the Western world:

> patrolling these areas, and stopping and searching contribute to a decrease in crime, while minority youths complain about harassment, do not trust the police and claim that institutions do not listen to their grievances. These grievances gave rise to riots and violence in France, and in Britain during the 1980s, 1990s and the 2000s, but specifically in 2005 in France and in 2011 in England, the United States experiencing less riots than criminal violence in inner cities.

There are relatively few comparative studies on policing, race/ethnicity, space, and the management of social order. This research is based on interviews with youths, police organizations, elected officials, and residents in the *banlieues* and inner cities in France, Britain, and the US. We were members of two independent commissions. In the first, *Groupe d'études et de luttes contre les discriminations* (2000–2003), we conducted a two-year seminar of research based on qualitative interviews with policemen of all ranks, experts on cities' problems and policy-makers in charge of such issues. We examined and analyzed all of the files from the toll-free number (114) open to victims of discrimination and the follow up given to their claims. In the second national commission, during our six years at the *Commission Nationale de Déontologie sur la Sécurité* (CNDS), we heard hundreds of testimonies from residents of inner cities claiming to have been victims of police and other law enforcer discrimination as well as the presumed authors of the wrong doing (policemen, counsels, lawyers, and mayors). We synthesized and made recommendations for each case at the national level as well. Another field study conducted among young people of immigrant background entering the French army completes our views on identities of second and third generations, and their experience with ethnic discrimination of the military institution. Our doctoral students leading field research on this topic have also enriched our approach to the issue. We analyze the contexts in which youth grievances turn into conflicts and confrontations.

DOI: 10.1057/9781137428004.0003

Despite apparent similarities, the controlled populations have different profiles in the three countries. In France and Britain, most are citizens of immigrant origin from former colonial empires; in the US, they belong to racial minorities. In the US and Britain, the awareness of their rights comes from a long experience of protest, channeled via organizations at either the community or the national level.

Solutions are rarely found in interactions with the police in France, where the national police are required to maintain order in peripheral neighborhoods. The young male populations living there frequently complain about ethnic profiling and the impunity benefiting public employees, even in the case of obvious discriminatory behaviors. They are seen by policemen as potential suspects, as idle male youths, even if the latter potential of violence is of low intensity. Policemen themselves have a discretionary power leaving them free to make choices. Dworkin calls this police discretion, 'the hole in the doughnut', in which discretion is the empty area in the middle of a ring of policies and procedures (Dworkin, 1977: 37). Yet despite such power, police officers feel despised by populations of inner cities and they lose their own self-esteem, complaining about the absence of support from their intermediary hierarchy, poor living standards, continuous reforms, changes in objectives, and a lack of proper initial and continuous training.

This unease is also perceived in the UK which represents a middle-way in terms of decentralization, attempting at the top to make officers more accountable, while in the US, the diversity of the 17,000 police forces, the contexts in which they operate and their various modes of policing yield more case by case schemes. The focus on large cities reveals that minority representation within police forces in the US, considered as a model for European countries, may differ but does not necessarily imply that tensions are less important in marginalized areas when a police chief is a minority member.

Anti-discrimination policies have been developing since the end of the 1990s following European and national agendas. European directives, national laws and cases have been examined by the European Court of Human Rights and by national courts. But police abuse, although not a current practice, is minimized, as in the US, where in courts the word of police officers is far more important than that of discriminated victims, although such events have become less frequent, with a stronger impact of court decisions and anti-discrimination policies.

DOI: 10.1057/9781137428004.0003

The main question of this research is how the police can be reformed and how each country tries to do so, offering more inclusive models and practices of citizenship. It is in each countries' interest to reform their police force and offer such models because the aforementioned youths are either current or future national citizens. One way to do it is by reflecting on racism and discrimination in inner cities where police culture is acquired on the job, and influenced by the practice of ethnic profiling, which sometimes mixes international and domestic security issues. Another approach is to examine whether the composition of the police force is reflective of multicultural populations, and if police-men with an immigrant or a minority background benefit from the same advancement opportunities and respect accorded to their "white" counterparts.

The treacherous nature of cross-national comparisons

Is a cross-national comparison possible on such issues? Does it make sense to attempt a comparison between a vast territorial, multiracial, and multiethnic world superpower with a relatively short history with two European nation-states molded by centuries of traditions, legal cultures, and political institutions (Body-Gendrot, 2012: 13)? This may be like comparing roses and peonies, yet it is done frequently within a long and well-established tradition emphasizing American "exceptionalism" (to quote Tocqueville, then Lipset (1996): each of us is in some ways like everybody else, in some ways like somebody else, and in some ways like nobody else. What is true of individuals is also true of countries and nations.

The US was created differently, and has to be understood on its own terms and within its own context. Its complex immigrant heritage, its long, checkered history of race relations, its political, institutional, and cultural responses to social challenges, all make this society a uniquely valuable source of insight and experience. It opens comparisons of commonalities and divergences with European countries, as pointed out by Marshall (1997: ix, 2001).

Without even mentioning the gaps occurring in data measurement, the misleading nature of comparisons cannot be minimized. To list just a few problems: comparing countries of different sizes and tracing parallel

DOI: 10.1057/9781137428004.0003

dimensions between a long past molded by regal power, then revolutions on one hand, and on the other, half a continent with a short history of law and order comprised of 50 states, may lead to oversimplification. The institutions are different. Furthermore, the nature and seriousness of violence sets the American experience apart. It is not simply a question of numbers. The crime rate is six or seven times higher than in Europe with variations according to the types of crime and places, namely inner cities. It is a question of the nature of crime. In the past, violence has been very much on the side of the forces of law and of the established citizens. Populism has resulted from the weakness of institutions. Menaces to social stability at various times in American history (the Frontier, the beginning of the industrial era, communities' evolution confronting massive immigration) have led "solid citizens" to ally to the cause of order and punitive communalism, and take the law into their own hands. The absence of a feudal past, the strength of the Protestant religion, the weakness of the central state characterize the US, leading to binary visions of the elected winners, the "deserving entitled," abiding by social conventions, and of the nondeserving losers. James Whitman (2003) points out the comparative harshness of American punishment and blames the absence of aristocratic codes of behavior which, in Europe, gradually granted offenders the treatment previously reserved for elite offenders, which is largely absent in the US (think of the French Director of the International Monetary Fund [IMF], handcuffed, shown on all televisions and sent to Rikkers Island in 2012 like any ordinary criminal).

Differences are also explained by other dimensions. Street crime linked to crack epidemics, gang warfare, and fights evoke the "American romance with guns" (Cole, 2012: 48). There are as many guns as people in America, according to estimates 45% of American households possess a gun. According to a Pew research poll, more Americans (49%) favor gun rights than gun control (45%) in 2012. It would be difficult not to draw a correlation with the number of violent deaths, including homicides in this country. Eight more blacks are killed by guns than whites, a statistic which raises the issue of race that will be developed below. The size of the incarcerated population, unique in the Western World with over two million people locked up and over five million under judicial supervision, along with the persistence of capital punishment are also unique features of American criminal law.

A major difference between France on one hand and on the other hand, the US and Britain, has to do with the nature of law. Two highly

DOI: 10.1057/9781137428004.0003

influential legal traditions characterize the Western world: civil law and common law. English and American laws are based on common law, that is, on tradition. Moreover, in the US, constitutional rights are the basis of American identity. By contrast, civil law in France dates back to the 13th century and after monarchy, was submitted to the Napoleonic Code which enunciated powerful, rigid administrative rules, hard to enforce, by comparison with the flexible rules of common law countries which were rigorously enforced (Tocqueville, 1961 6, 14).

Following Lijphart (1999), one should distinguish consensual (or socio-democratic corporatist) countries such as France, Germany, and the Scandinavian countries in Europe—from majoritarian, neo-liberal, conflictual democracies (the majorities dictate the choices, they are also more populist) including Anglophone countries such as Britain and the US Consensual democracies are more welfare-friendly, more prone to trade-offs and moderate criminal policies, relying on a lenient "culture of excuse." Majoritarian democracies express more severity, more punishment to the alleged nondeserving (Lappi-Seppala, 2011). Procedures and/or images referring to law and order issues reveal what is embedded in the subconscious of societies. In contrast with the US, there may be less absolute respect for rules of procedures, and less litigiousness in Europe. Punitive populism and the harshness of sanctions are not as exacerbated as they may be in parts of the US, both in rhetoric and in practice. The fact that judges are not elected makes them less prone to political pressures than is the case in parts of the US where the harshness of punishment is not considered as unequal treatment (Body-Gendrot and Savitch, 2012: 15–16). The rules of common law are like the rules of a game that is constantly readjusted. Politicians, police, and judges are accountable to the people who appoint or elect them. They have to find a rationale and empirical regulations to conflicts of interests emanating from heterogeneous individuals or communities. Conversely, in France, law is conceived as part of a transcendental sphere (Garapon, 1996). Those who say, interpret, repair or enforce the law are seen as invested in a symbolic action at the demand of a political body. Their role is to strengthen the link between the people and a social, political, philosophical contract above them that has been disrupted by violence or crime.

In the US and in the UK, the role of the state should remain limited to emergency situations (i.e., the rescue of banks, protectionism). The state is not at the foundation of collective identity or solidarity, as it is in France. Citizenship is not a recurring national debate. National intervention in social processes in order to redress inequalities is perceived as suspicious as it implies a form of socialism, contrary to the ideology of laissez-faire (Body-Gendrot and Savitch, 2012: 14). Only 16% of Americans support such an intervention versus 75% to 80% of the French, depending on the year (Gallup, 2011). What the French *think* ideologically (on the right/on the left) is more important in the definition of their identity than what they *are*.

However, in societies where the recognition of differences in identity prevail, anti-discriminatory policies based on the legitimacy of minorities' rights, and on equal opportunity are supported by majorities. They encourage the search for solutions via a pluralism of public actors, firms, and third sector parties in various forms of governance. In the three countries, research shows that correlations exist between racial/visible minorities, poverty, single-parent families, school drop-outs, disinvested urban zones and potential crime, and collective disorders calling for police surveillance. But where negative perceptions correlate them with racial minorities in the US, they do so with the former African and Arab immigrants, in France and with both racial minorities and newly arrived immigrants in the UK. Such generalizations need to be reviewed according to other factors such as class, age, gender, location, time of settlement, and so on.

The institutional recognition of racism

Another difficulty of this research has to do with the institutional recognition, be it accorded, or not, to racism. While there has been an explosion of writing on theoretical debates related to race and racism, French scholars have been slow to come forward and join these discussions, with certain significant exceptions. A pioneer, Colette Guillaumin, published a seminal work in 1972, *L'idéologie raciste: génèse et langage actuel* (Guillaumin, 1972). In the same trend, Véronique De Rudder and her colleagues worked on inter-ethnic relations (1991) while Daniele Lochak reflected on the concept of discrimination, offering a legal point of view on what could be done to protect foreign migrants from unfair practices (Lochak, 1992. In 1988, Pierre-André Taguieff published *La force du préjugé. Essai sur le racisme et ses doubles*, a major edited book. That very same year, E. Balibar, in a dialogue with I. Wallerstein, pointed out that a major difference opposed France and the US in their models

DOI: 10.1057/9781137428004.0003

of immigrant and minority integration: while Americans promoted the ethnicization of minorities, France, perceiving itself as an ethnically homogeneous country, promoted the ethnicity of majorities (Balibar and Wallerstein, 1988: 20).

But one must acknowledge that there has been a general reluctance to discuss racism among French intellectuals who saw the issue through the historical lens of anti-semitism. In 1992, during a meeting of French social scientists, the use of the term *race* was heavily discussed. Being devoid of substance, should it be removed from the French Constitution? Some scientists argued that even if racism was real, the concept of race was unscientific. Nevertheless, there was no insistence on the need to "ban" the term, and studies of race continued to emerge in France. Because of the French history of ethnicized religious strife, the racial quotas imposed to on Jews during World War Two, and the explicitly racist legislation in Algeria and other French colonies, there is a historic wariness on the part of public officials to deploy racial categories, especially when fighting ethnic and racial discriminations. A popular French mode of thinking was expressed by former President Pompidou, asserting that merely mentioning a term calls for the idea and then makes it reality. While French scholars did, indeed, recognize that complex identities, including racial ones, are constructed through time and place, individually and collectively (Hall, 1991), this acknowledgment occupied a minor position compared with debates on inequalities, poverty, and social justice. Racism in France came to be understood broadly, to include "any form of violence exerted against another human group, from prejudice and/or contempt to discrimination; from segregation to random or organized murder," thus, as any form of hostility toward a designated group (e.g., anti-youth, anti-cops, etc.) (Guillaumin, 1994: 67–68). An illustration of this particularly French designation applies to conflicts between youths and police forces in low income and immigrant neighborhoods. This is the object of this study. It is only very recently, in 2012, that a dictionary with hundreds of items recapitulated various forms of historical and critical approaches to racism (Taguieff, 2012). Still, countries such as the US and the UK have given recognition to *institutional racism* which uncovers and exposes ideological and political racism buried in the practices and institutional cultures of housing, work, school, health, and police work; and they have attempted to redress these problems. In contrast, France remains silent on questions of potential

DOI: 10.1057/9781137428004.0003

institutional racism. Unions protect public employees and strongly resist debates on racism in general. As Poli (2001: 198) observed in France, "the first reaction to questions related to racism is silence." Currently, however, there is an agreement that the concept needs to be qualified. There is an emerging consensus around the idea of race as a "political object referring to boundaries between social inclusion and exclusion" (Balibar, 2005: 14–15) and to rights and legitimate grievances.

Finally, the term "inner city" needs some clarification. While referring to the studies of the sociologists of the School of Chicago in the 1920s, the inner city in the US is historically close to the business district—that is, at the core of the city. With the improvement of transportation, the gentry consistently relocated to more amenable suburbs which, after the 1920s, grew twice as fast as central cities; in Britain, rich and poor areas were less clearly delimitated inside of cities, public housing was less architecturally massive and poor households have dwelled in private housing as well. In France, *banlieue* designates, theoretically, an urbanized area on the outskirts of a large city. But as used by the media and in popular discourse, the term refers to urban deprivation, illiteracy, segregation, poverty, drugs and crime; the subtext, as with the inner city, being that large, dependent *immigré* families are concentrated in massive public housing estates, living from public aid and being the source of urban problems (Body-Gendrot, 2009; Fourcaut, Bellanger, and Flonneau, 2007). It is this stigmatized and criminalized sense which is used here when referring to the inner city as it connects with both disorder and policing.

The complexity of making cross-cultural comparisons is a bulwark against simplistic universalism—the assumption that "what works" in one context will work in another. As stated by Manning (2005: 30), epistemological virtues of comparison allow the transcendence of American parochialism and ethnocentrism. This remark applies to other countries as well. Specific cases reveal the social and contingent nature of knowledge, and of its difficult transmission to practices. A careful comparison may yield real insight.

The extent of knowledge in social sciences has changed enormously over the course of the last three decades. We now know much more than we used to. We have sufficient comparative data on crime and law and order, and the quality of this data is continuously improving. We have enough evidence to test (or at least disconfirm) various circulating

DOI: 10.1057/9781137428004.0003

theories (Body-Gendrot and Savitch, 2012: 18). In other words, we have gained the opportunity to exploit the naturally occurring differences between countries and, thus, to attempt to do innovative comparative research.

This comparative research aims at starting a debate which has as much to do with delinquency and police practices as with the nature of the state.

DOI: 10.1057/9781137428004.0003

2
Contexts of Grievances

Abstract: *France is an old immigration country. In 1974, the settlement of immigrant families as a result of the end of the recruit of North African labor force led to a strong politicization of immigration in the political discourse and to conflicts between police forces and the so-called second generation in a context where immigration was not still considered as a permanent element of French populations and identity. In Britain, the 14% minority population accounts for 80% of the population growth. Fears focus on Muslims after terrorist attacks and they are accentuated by inflows from beleaguered countries and Eastern Europe. Youths and police antagonisms have simmered in cities and the police have had the task of containing and constraining them. In the US, the American dilemma is not citizenship but race. The relationship of minorities and the police has been improved after minorities mobilized on issues of discrimination and brutality. More minorities were hired in the last decades and community policing smoothed relationships in some cities.*

Body-Gendrot, Sophie and Catherine Wihtol de Wenden. *Policing the Inner City in France, Britain, and the US.* New York: Palgrave Macmillan, 2014. DOI: 10.1057/9781137428004.0004.

The case of France

Historical background

France is an old immigration country, the oldest in Europe, it has always hesitated between a policy of settlement and a policy of labor force. At first, the shortage of workers and future soldiers in the second part of the 19th century led to the call for foreign workers. The scope was to produce French citizens out of a foreign workforce in spite of public debates which were focused on the risks of immigration for French identity. In 1974, a turning point occurred when France decided to stop the recruitment of a salaried labor force. This decision, initially provisional, stopped the mobility of foreigners between France and their countries of origin, and defined a policy of integration. In the 1980s, a strong politicization of immigration and integration took place, with the rise of Le Pen at local elections of 1983. Immigration, which was formerly a topic of low politics, became a stake of high politics. The revival of republican values, largely forgotten in the past "Trente Glorieuses" (30 prosperous years of growth after World War II) came then on the forefront. One of the French paradoxes lies in the fact that there has been more political controversy between the left and right about the control of immigration flows, for which most of the decision making is, however, decided in Brussels than about the management of stocks (integration) which is rather consensual in France, but for which France has a full sovereignty of decision. Another paradox is that the French model of republican integration is more contested abroad than its policy of border control, contrarily to French political debates. This paradox has given a strong role to the police forces in their role function of maintaining the internal order in a centralized country where the state has always had the upper hand.

Since 1982, the figures of statistics for foreigners in France have been stabilized around three to five million foreigners and four to five million immigrants (6% to 9% of total population), a distinction introduced in the census of 1999. Foreigners are those who are not French. Immigrants are those who were born abroad and who have physically gone to France even if they have got French citizenship. But the composition of immigration has changed. Since the census of 1975, Europeans have ceased to be the majority (Italians, Portuguese, Spanish, Yugoslavs) and the presence of non-Europeans has increased: Maghrebians, Sub-Saharians, with

DOI: 10.1057/9781137428004.0004

a strong rise of Moroccans and Tunisians. While Algerian populations have declined, figures for Turkish, Sub-Saharan Africans, and Asians are steadily increasing. The discontinuation of immigration after the first oil shock has facilitated family reunification. Many immigrants who were moving in-and-out across borders have become permanent settlers with their families. Their children were born abroad, arriving very young in France or were born in France and obtained French citizenship at the majority of 18 years old, in most cases, or the day of their birth for Algerian children born in France from parents also born in France when Algeria was part of France (before 1963). Therefore, the second generations appeared earlier than in other European countries. In 1990: urban policies (*politique de la ville*), founded on the territorialization of public intervention in selected zones of social exclusion, without referring to ethnicity, were launched, followed by years of debates on the reform of the nationality code on citizenship, identity and nationality founded more so on jus soli or jus sanguinis. Then, in 2005, the riots of November in some inner cities of Ile de France, like Clichy sous-Bois, legitimized debates on police and inner city populations.

Questioning nationality and citizenship

Although France was the largest immigration country in Europe between 1880 and 1970, this reality has first been unknown, difficultly accepted, and submitted to controversies between the state, employers, public opinion, and various political trends, from nationalists to liberals of the right and left. National identity has never been defined by immigration because it has been built on the myth of ethnic homogeneity of the population, on the philosophy of the social contract and the political community of citizens. Newcomers were considered as individuals having to disappear in a predefined political model, and had to abandon their differences upon entry.

The so-called "Trente Glorieuses" (1945–1974) opened a long period of attempts to design an immigration policy. The new needs of the labor force for reconstruction after the World War II, the pressure of employers in the sectors of housing, agriculture, and industry had rapidly set the tone after a short period when the Government tried to master the situation. Rapidly the employers took the initiative to go themselves to the countries of origin and illegally recruit an immigrant labor force, for a short time and without families. These young and male workers were, then, legalized by the administration (around 200,000 per year).

DOI: 10.1057/9781137428004.0004

The Minister of Labor, in charge of immigration, thought immigration was temporary and that immigrants were determined to return to their home country. Public declarations by De Gaulle, Pompidou, and some ministers of Labor (like Gorse, Jeanneney) show that immigration was considered as a means to reduce social pressure and to respond to the demands of labor, in a short-term approach. The public authorities tried to separate this question from the great debates of the period (Industrial policy, Planning, Reconstruction, Housing, Growth, Algerian war, May 1968), keeping immigration out of political struggles. When Valery Giscard d'Estaing was elected as President of the Republic (1974–1981), the government decided to stop immigration: the oil crisis, the rise of unemployment, the influence of similar decisions taken in 1973 in Germany, Netherlands, and Belgium, and the unilateral decision of Algeria to put an end to its immigration explain this major turning point.

The year 1981 presented many possibilities. The law of October 9, 1981 on the freedom of associations by foreigners replaced the former authorization of the Home ministry by a declaration of association at this ministry. The law of October 17, 1981 on entry and settlement modified the ordinance of 1945, confirming the cessation of labor immigration but protecting foreigners against the abuse of the administration. It sanctioned employers of undocumented workers, and struggled against illegal migration while reinforcing the legal status of those settled in France. Some categories of foreigners like the "second generations" born in France and staying there, long-term residents, foreigners married with French, and parents of French children, benefitted from a consolidated stay.

The walk for equality and against discrimination called the "Marche des beurs" (the March of Arabs), which gathered second generation immigrants of North African descent who walked from Marseilles to Paris with a triumphal arrival on December 1, 1983, has inspired the second left law adopted unanimously by the Parliament on August 17, 1984: the law automatically granting the ten year residence card on the criteria of residence, automatically renewable to some categories of foreigners: foreigners married with French, parents of French children, and residents in France for more than 15 years. This card grants access to to all occupations without any restriction of job or of territory. This step has been considered as one of the most successful gains of the associative movement. While foreigners had obtained the equality of social rights since 1975, the consciousness that immigrants are not only workers but

DOI: 10.1057/9781137428004.0004

also settlers begins to appear even if their access to local citizenship is postponed after having been written in the Common platform of the left in 1981.

The disturbances brought by the first Gulf war (1991) in civic "beur" (Arab) associations question the Government about the allegiances of the second generation youths, but the strong associations' movement which struggle for loyalty with the French Government involvement in the Gulf war after war takes over. Meanwhile, Charles Pasqua, the Home Minister, introduced a law reforming the nationality code in a restrictive way, after years of debates on French identity, in 1993. In 1995, terrorism struck in Paris: two attacks killed commuters in the RER (regional express railway) and the radical Muslim Khaled Kelkal, who put bombs on the Train à grande vitesse (TGV) tracks in Lyons surroundings, was killed by policemen. In 1996, illegal sub-Saharans on hunger strikes for their legalization in the St Bernard church in Paris in la Goutte d'or in the 18th district are pursued on August 26th (on the anniversary of the declaration of Human Rights and Citizenship of 1789) by the police who broke the door of the church. The symbol is very powerful.

At the end of the century, at Sangatte, a small village where the tunnel under the Channel was built, thousands of undocumented migrants gathered with the hope of reaching the UK by boat, lorry, or train. They originated from Afghanistan, Pakistan, Iran, Iraq and they had family or regional links with the Pakistanis and other countrymen settled in UK. The left Government seems to fear the National Front and public opinion and does not make any decision about immigrant flows.

Another debate in this context is the access to nationality, considered as a tool of the assimilation policy. The French model of access to nationality is built on an equilibrium between "jus sanguinis" and "jus soli." The French law on nationality was inspired by the civil code of Napoleon I in 1804 which substituted the "jus sanguinis" to the former "jus soli" inherited from the Ancient regime (attachment of the peasant to the land of his owner). In 1889, an important reform of the nationality law introduced an essential aspect of "jus soli" to those born in France. The lawmakers enlarged it in the reforms of 1927, 1945, and 1973. No political debates had arisen from such reforms because the nationality code was not a political issue and citizenship was an outmoded topic compared with class struggles in the 1970s. But this rapidly changed under the pressure of the extreme right in the mid-1980s. During this period, the National Front and its think tank, the Club de l'Horloge

DOI: 10.1057/9781137428004.0004

(the Clock Club), launched a new debate on French identity with the title "Etre français, cela se mérite" (one deserves to be French) and "les Français de papier" (those who are French only via their identity cards but not in their minds). They implied that the French of foreign origin (the so-called "second generations") had no desire to be French against their will ("Français malgré eux"). This notion referred symbolically to inhabitants of the former Alsace-Lorraine territory during the two World Wars who were enlisted, in spite of themselves, in the German army. The question of nationality and citizenship rapidly became a question of high politics, intensifying debates on identity (what does it mean to be French?), allegiances, and loyalty. The Left answered with a book on *Identité française* (1985), showing that it refused to abandon the debate on French identity and citizenship to the extreme right. The impact on public opinion (the *Figaro magazine* has published an issue on November 1985 on: "Serons-nous encore Français dans trente ans?") (Will we still be French in the next 30 years?) led the Chirac Government to appoint in 1987 a Commission of Experts (*Commission des Sages*) to decide on a reform of the French nationality code. Headed by the high civil servant Marceau Long, the vice president of the State Council (the highest administrative court), the commission proceeded to a hundred hearings. In the end, paradoxically, the definition of French identity was inversed between right and left, referring to their historical credos. The right defended a definition of French nationality based on the social contract and the collective will to live together (arguments defended by Rousseau's social contract and Ernest Renan's discourse on "*Qu'est ce qu'une nation?*"—what is a nation?—in 1871), while the left adopted the theme of socialization by residency, stressing the importance of the soil, in terms used by the right in late 19th century by rightist ideologists such as Maurice Barrès. The debate also led many second generations to feel better in light of their French identity instead of questioning it and to require their papers proving their French nationality under the threat of a refer restricting its access. Left associations such as the League for Human Rights, the Mouvement Contre le Racisme et pour l'Egalité des Peuples (MRAP), SOS Racism were much opposed to a reform which would suppress the automatic access to French nationality for foreign children. Many dual nationals became convinced by the theme of "citizenship of residence" introduced by civic associations. No decision was taken at the eve of new presidential election of 1988.

DOI: 10.1057/9781137428004.0004

After several years of debates a new law was passed on July 22, 1993 (*the Pasqua Méhaignerie law*) when the right came back to power. The law suppressed the automatic access to French nationality at 18 years old for those born in France of foreign parents and having continuously lived in France for five years: young foreigners accessing French nationality at their majority had to make a request to a judge. Young people convicted of penalties exceeding six months could not have access to French nationality. This law was inspired from the themes on the national Front platform. When the left came back to power in 1997, a new law (called *Guigou law*) in 1998 came back to the former equilibrium between "jus soli" and "jus sanguinis," suppressing the will to become French at 18 and restoring the automatic access to French nationality at the majority for those born in France from foreign parents.

Questioning integration

France is considered by many foreign observers as an assimilationist and centralized country, led by a strong state and by Jacobinist (centralized) and republican values which are required to be accepted by newcomers. They are supposed to abandon their collective behaviors in the public space. The reality is more complex. France has always been a multicultural country built on internal diversities (the so-called "provinces" of the Ancient regime). At the eve of the 1789 revolution, there were still many diversities in the French kingdom, namely a strong autonomy of regional parliaments set against the royal power. During the revolution, the "Girondins" (those for decentralizaton) failed against the "Jacobins" (for centralization) in their effort to preserve regional autonomies. The revolution and then the first Empire went on to unify and strengthen the administrative powers and laws creating geographical "départements" to break regionalisms, elaborating civil (1804) and criminal law codes, and then, during the third republic, making public school compulsory, free of charge and secularized (1884) and establishing a military draft for all (1908). The definition of the citizen by the declaration of Human rights of 1789 and the universal suffrage in 1848 for all men contributed to build the feeling of a common political culture from Rousseau's *Contrat social*, the "*Vive la nation*" shouted at the battle of Valmy (1792) and Ernest Renan's "Vouloir vivre collectif" in his dissertation on "*Qu'est-ce qu'une nation?*" Other public initiatives such as the invention of a common collective imaginary (the national holiday of July 14th (Bastille Day) in 1889 during the third Republic, the building of statues of Marianne and

DOI: 10.1057/9781137428004.0004

of the Republic, the urban creations of squares and avenues holding the name of the Republic or of Alsace Lorraine, the provinces lost after the defeat of Sedan, in 1870, the war memorials after World War I in each of the 36,000 communes of France and its colonies), all these contributed to cancel or weaken ethnic feelings in modern France and impose an ethnicization of majorities.

Yet some regionalisms appeared in late 19th century. It was first a traditional defense of local culture. But lately in the move of May 1968, regionalism became a left-wing claim Corsica keeps leading a separatist fight against France and has obtained some recognition with the creation, some twenty years ago, of a University at Corte where the Corsican language is taught. A Corsican parliamentary Assembly was created in 2002. But the acceptance of a *peuple corse* has been defined in 1991 as contrary to the French Constitution, according to the Constitutional Council on May 9, 1991 while an armed faction goes on with terrorism at local level. This same High Court also condemned the European Charter of Regional and Minority languages as contrary to the republican principles of the republic in 1999 and reasserted the unicity of the French. However, there are many exceptions to these rules in French overseas territories: polygamy is commonly practiced in Mayotte, there are three kings in Polynesia, and secularism is reluctantly respected in those areas.

Lingering paradoxes

However, France is considered abroad as an old fashioned, assimilationist, and sovereignist country and many observers are debating on "*intégration à la française.*" While in the 60s, the term "assimilation" had still been maintained, since 1980 in the public discourse on inclusion policy, the term "integration," already used at the end of the French presence in colonial Algeria, was introduced in 1974 by the new State Secretary on immigration appointed by Valery Giscard d'Estaing, Paul Dijoud. The idea was to abandon a too individualistic and authoritarian approach in favor of the expression of cultural diversities in order to help foreigners to go back home while maintaining a common culture. Languages and cultures of origin were taught at school to children of foreigners in 1974. Some other public terms were used, such as "insertion," a functionalist definition of integration reduced to the main tools to live in France used by Lionel Stoleru, a State Secretary to (on) immigration, and "Living together" ("*Vivre ensemble*") by the Minister of Social Affairs, Georgina

DOI: 10.1057/9781137428004.0004

Dufoix in 1983. Some civic associations in the move of the beur (second generation) movement born with the "Marche des beurs" of 1983 (SOS Racisme and France Plus, born both in 1984) tried to develop the notion of the right to "difference" (SOS Racisme), then to "indifference" (France Plus). The emphasis put on Islam gave some specificity to the French approach of integration: the scarf affair of 1989 and then the law of 2004 prohibiting the wearing of ostentatious religious signs in public schools stressed secularism as a republican value to be shared by future citizens, while other emblematic values have disappeared (the military draft has been terminated by Jacques Chirac in 1995) and the value of fraternity is seriously challenged by the "social gap" ("*la fracture sociale*," a term used by Jacques Chirac during his presidential campaign in 1995). The debate on the mention of origins in the statistics of the French to improve the evaluation of ethnic discriminations has been abandoned. Public opinion does not seem to be ready for such a turning point in the French definition of citizenship.

A territorial approach, the urban policy

The most original policy of integration in France is less the hesitations between assimilation, integration, insertion, or plural citizenship than its territorial approach of the treatment of differences, implemented in social terms because France does not recognize any ethnic group. A first break in the unitary ideology has been the positive discrimination approach, based on social criteria introduced in 1981 with the priority zones of education ZEP ("*Zones d'éducation prioritaire*") in districts where children are experiencing cumulated social discriminations, in order to fight against social exclusion at school. During the 80s, under the pressures of several left mayors, several measures of prevention against urban violence were integrated in the program of urban social development ("*développement social des quartiers*"). Several districts were included as experimental sites in this territorialization of public intervention, leading to the so-called "policy of the city." In 1990, a Ministry of the City was created. Based on a territorialization of zones of social poverty, such urban policy fights against exclusion. Ethnicity is never mentioned, nor affirmative action: these two terms remain a taboo in this country of formal equality of rights. In order to maintain social cohesion in districts with high rates of unemployment among the parents and the "second generations," since the mid-80s, subsidies have been allocated to civic associations to maintain social cohesion and to fight against urban

DOI: 10.1057/9781137428004.0004

violence. A contractual policy has been created between municipalities with problem inner cities and the Ministry of the City (214 "contrats de ville" in 1994). In 1996, the relaunching of this urban policy by Prime Minister Alain Juppé defined 751 problem zones (zones urbaines sensibles, ZUS) which legitimized territorialized public interventions. In 1999, 1300 districts and six million were involved in the city contacts ("contrats de ville"). In early 2008, the State Secretary to the City, Fadela Amara, the former president of the association "*Ni Putes ni soumises*" (Neither Whores nor Submitted) appointed by Nicolas Sarkozy launched a new plan stressing reinforced police of proximity, monitoring at school and help for finding jobs. In 2010, 750 "zones urbaines sensibles" (sensitive urban zones) (ZUS) representing 4.5 million inhabitants were included in the policy of the City, and 911 ZEP (zones d'éducation prioritaire) representing 20% of the school students in France and 85 ZFU ("zones franches urbaines": free enterprise zones for the settlement of firms, free from taxes in exchange of the creation of local employment). The Minister of the City under the Presidency of François Hollande between 2012 and 2014, François Lamy, redefined the positive actions of public intervention in discriminated zones, stressing more poverty and less taboo ethnic discriminations and including a lot of rural areas in the program. He put an end to the so-called ZUS ("Zones urbaines sensibles") with his creation of one thousand "Quartiers prioritaires" (priority areas) with only one criterion kept, that of poverty. He also tried to sanction discrimination exerted via stigmatized geographical residence ("discrimination à l'adresse"). In some inner cities, the mayors are elected with hardly 30% of votes, due to massive abstention and to the presence of foreigners deprived from voting rights (Kepel, 2012). The political elites are cut from their constituencies. They are pleading for more participative democracy.

Partnerships between the state, the municipalities and the firms have been undertaken. The municipalization of public policy led to a municipalization of many former associative activists, included in city partnerships: cultural mediators, ethnic leaders were granted delegations of competences from the top of the state and from municipalities for the management of urban, social, and cultural projects at the grass root level. Many associations collaborated more with municipalities as partners than with the state, which led them to focus their actions on localism, fighting against exclusion and violence more than helping the populations living there to move out with a goal of upward social

DOI: 10.1057/9781137428004.0004

mobility. Some activists also encouraged local participation, citizenship of residence, a political project rooted in participative democracy and citizenship but which did not help the populations to get rid of determinisms linked to those inner cities" (Body-Gendrot and Wihtol de Wenden, 2007).

There is a conflict between two republican ideals in urban policy and citizenship. A first trend is a meritocratic approach consisting of helping the young and poor elite from inner cities to get rid of the tyranny of their territories of residence, by giving them a chance to live elsewhere via a social individual mobility. This model was used in the countryside during the Third Republic. The second model consists of reinforcing democracy and participation in inner cities, thanks to associations, firms, and mediators but with a population staying there, expecting to plant deeper roots in local democracy. This is another republican project. Both practices exist in France without a clear choice. The emphasis on long-term housing policies rather than on the populations has reinforced the second option, creating a number of relegated districts (Thuot, 2013).

Islam

The recognition of Islam is another pillar of the French integration policy. France has the largest population of Muslims (between five and six million but they are not counted as such by the census). Most of them are of Maghrebin origin (Algerians, Moroccans, and Tunisians), including 500,000 *harkis* and their families (who fought on the French side during the Algerian war) and second or third generations of French. The presence of Islam began to emerge in French public space in the mid-80s when they began to address collective claims: strikes in the car industry in 1984 mixing working-class and religious mobilization in collective housing for foreign workers asking for prayer rooms, and in local places when they required specific areas in the churchyards, visible mosques in the urban landscape, hallal meat slaughtering places and markets.

The scarves in public schools in 1989 opened the debate on the compatibility of Islam with republican secularist values. Islam is seen mainly in France as the religion of the poor, the colonized. Its elites are not visible. It meets many forms of rejection in public opinion. In order to settle some dialogue with religious leaders and to manage Islam within the secularized rules, two Home Ministers have tried to set structures of dialogue and of representation. Nicolas Sarkozy launched, in 2002, the CFCM (*Conseil français du culte musulman*). Inside the CFCM,

DOI: 10.1057/9781137428004.0004

the legitimacy of the main associations of Islam in France is a matter of controversy because the criteria have been the square meters of prayer rooms granted by associations. This decision has given more influence to big associations subsidized by Saudi Arabia such as the UOIF (*Union des organizations islamiques de France*) or by Morocco like the FNMF (*Fédération Nationale des Musulmans de France*) than to smaller associations financed by Muslim families. For years, the attitude of the Home Ministries has been traditionally to privilege partnership with the Rector of the Great Mosque of Paris, built in 1926 to thank Muslim fighters involved in World War I. With others, they conquered the Douaumont Fort in 1916, near Verdun. This mosque first depended on the French Government in Algiers and, after independence, Algeria appointed the former rector of the Paris mosque, Hamza Boubaker, who had previously been appointed by France in Algiers.

His son, Dalil Boubaker, the present Rector, who is a French and Algerian bi-national, was appointed by Algeria. He shares republican values with the Home Ministry and he is considered as a man of dialogue and compromise. The institutionalized dialogue has not prevented France from controversial conflicts, namely about scarves in public schools. After the initial decision of the State Council prohibiting the wearing of ostentatious signs of religious belonging in schools, a law along these same lines was passed on March 15, 2004. The law seems to have settled the question. In 2011, a new law was passed prohibiting the burka (total veil covering the body) in the public space.

Anti-discrimination policy

It has taken a long time for France to include this public policy into the credo of equality of rights. The definition of citizenship built on formal equality in the declaration of 1789 ("*Tous les hommes naissent libres et égaux en droits*") has delayed the perception of effective inequalities built on ethnic and religious discriminations. The first law against racism was voted in France in 1972, thanks to the MRAP (*Mouvement contre le Racisme et pour l'Amitié entre les peuples*), close to the Communist party. Article 13 of the Amsterdam treaty of the European Union in 1997 required France to implement public policy against discrimination with two new laws in 2001 and 2002. A light organization, the GED (*Groupe d'Etude des discriminations*), born in 1999 and rapidly changed into the GELD (*Groupe d'Etudes et de Luttes contre les discriminations*) was created under the auspices of the ministry of Social Affairs, Martine Aubry. In 2000, it

DOI: 10.1057/9781137428004.0004

experienced a free telephone number, the 114 to welcome and to deal with the victims of discriminations. Most of them were complaining about discrimination at work and by the police. The prefectures received the files with the complaints. But very few claims were brought to the courts and none concerning the police. In 2003, the GELD was terminated. Meanwhile, a *Commission nationale de deontologie sur la Securité* (Police Complaints National Commission), the CNDS, was created by the law of June 6, 2000, with an independent status, headed by the former president of the Highest Court of Justice (the Cassation Court), Pierre Truche, in order to combat institutional abuse from security forces (police, prisons, army during the repatriations) via contradictory hearings of victims and security forces. The annual reports addressed to the President of the Republic stressed ethnic discrimination by the police toward French of Arab, Black or Roma origins: a taboo in the French administration. Two laws were passed, in 2001, on discrimination at work following a research report at the initiative of the CFDT trade union and sociologist Philippe Bataille; and in 2002 on racist practices from employers. These laws require law enforcement officers to bring evidence that they have not practiced any indirect forms of discrimination. In 2004, another independent authority was created, the HALDE (*Haute autorité pour la lutte contre les discriminations et pour l'égalité*), headed by a high ranking civil servant, Louis Schweitzer, the former President of the Renault car industry. But its existence, weakly mediatized, remained largely ignored before its inclusion in the competences of the Defender of Rights. In the sphere of work, public policies supported, in 2007, the adoption of a Chart on Diversity to provide incentives for large firms to employ young people from diverse origins. The term "diversity" is now used in schools and universities, public housing, and, local and national political representation as an objective to strive for. In France, it refers more to the fight against social exclusion than to ethnic recognition. Nothing was done regarding police discriminatory practices.

Thirty years of debates on local political rights to non-Europeans

After 30 years of debates, the local voting rights of foreigners have still not been granted. Fifteen European countries have granted these rights to their non-European foreigners. The left program of the socialist candidate François Mitterrand, in 1981, promised local voting rights and eligibility to all foreigners along with the freedom of association, granted in 1981. François Mitterrand often repeated, during his long mandate

DOI: 10.1057/9781137428004.0004

(1981–1995), that he was in favor of such a reform but that public opinion was not ready for it. It was not until the modification of Article 3 of the Constitution which foresees that the voters in local elections participate in the designation of the electoral group which in turn proceeds to the election of the senators. So, foreigners would share national sovereignty which belongs to the French people, according to the Constitution ("*La souveraineté nationale appartient au peuple français*"). After years of internal debates inside of the socialist party, it was decided under the Jospin Government (1997–2002) to abandon the project due to fear of increasing the extreme right vote. In 2002, a bill was proposed by the green party at the National Assembly but it was not voted by the Senate. In 2012, François Hollande included local voting rights for foreigners in his 50th proposal for the presidential election. But the project seems to have been once more abandoned. The argument that it would bring an ethnic vote, an Arab vote or a Muslim vote possibly leading to their leadership at the head of municipalities has been weakened by the experiences of second and third generations who tend to vote like French citizens. Polls reveal that they follow the same voting trends as French citizens, although slightly more on the left, more abstentionist and also more conservative in their private values than their native French counterparts but without any political communautarism.

France is among the last European countries of immigration to give such restricted access to political mandates to the French of foreign origin: there are few MPs at the French National Assembly, at the Senate, and at the European Parliament, and local councilors are ordinarily assigned to the policy of the city in their municipalities and never at finances or at international affairs. Compared with the UK, the Netherlands, or Germany, the issue of political inclusion illustrate the reluctance of the French policy of political inclusion. During the riots in the autumn of 2005 in Clichy-sous-Bois and in other municipalities of the Paris outskirts, the feeling of low inclusion was largely shared by this population holding French citizenship. Most of the young rioters felt that they were not considered as fully French, that the republican values did not apply to them. They did not claim collective or identity recognition—not for a better place for Islam in France; they only requested equal rights.

Most immigration policy in France has been decided at the national level, with a strong impact of the republican inspiration, partially influenced and bargained with the most influent immigrant group, the

DOI: 10.1057/9781137428004.0004

Maghrebians and their sons who have given the tune: during the "beur" (Arab) association period, when integration policy was negotiated at the presidential palace, with civic associations, during the first Gulf war when they were called by the summits of the state to ensure the loyalty of the militants, at the eve of each presidential election because of the fantasy of an ethnic vote, in spite of exclusion and discrimination.

The security concern, with the progressive criminalization of illegal immigration in the early 1990s, September 11, 2001, and following the terrorist attacks in Europe, have led to more identity controls in the streets and more amalgamations between Islam, illegal status, delinquency, and terrorism. In many cases, this concern has provoked the toughest arguments in favor of security and adopted symbolic policies to reassure public opinion. At the local level, the share of responsibilities between the Ministry of the city, municipalities, social actors and associations has been more confused because it varies according to each specific case. The reluctance of the Home Ministry to take into account the discriminations practiced by some policemen in the daily life of many young people of foreign origin is coupled with the scarce attention given to the geographic and social mobility of inner city residents, in spite of a general consensus between the left and the right on integration. Integration is rarely discussed, except in passionate debates. The short-term solutions always prevail on long-term decisions, along with the pressures of public opinion and election agendas.

Britain

Unlike France, which accumulates constitutions, or the US, which has only one, the oldest functioning constitution, the British "unwritten constitution" is a collection of parliamentary acts, accepted conventions about the political process, and some judicial decisions, reinterpreted with relative ease according to circumstances (Schain, 2008: 120). In contrast with the Supreme Court in the US or the constitutional council in France, checking the constitutionality of laws passed by the other branches, the British Parliament is sovereign. The Executive branch controls the legislative agenda without constitutional constraints over governmental action. The Executive, at the centre of power, is not as much heavily influenced by lobbies as in the US nor by civil servants as in France, it is, however, dominated by partisan policymaking.

DOI: 10.1057/9781137428004.0004

Historical backgrounds

There has never been agreement about the definition of British, or even English identity. According to Rose (1982: 14), most people in the UK identify as English, Welsh, Scottish, or Irish rather than British. After World War II, this matter of identity was made more complex by a notion of citizenship which incorporated the whole population of the British Empire. As long as Britain was embedded within the Empire, and as there was no explicit citizenship, this did not matter much (Schain, 2008: 141). But subsequent legislations culminating in the 1981 *Nationality Act*, redefined what the rights of the residents from the former Empire, specifically from the New Commonwealth, the 8% of the population from Pakistan, India and the Caribbean who are non-white as opposed to those from Canada, Australia, and New Zealand) would be, revealing a certain number of paradoxes. The right to enter and stay was not granted to all nationals, while some non-nationals (with a British mother, for instance) had access to it. Citizens from the Commonwealth whose entry and stay were controlled and limited were granted civil rights and even voting rights, even though they were non-nationals, once they had been authorized to enter the UK. Lastly, legislation on immigration reorganized in 1971, 1983, and 1988 molded the legislation relative to nationality, by contrast with France. "There (was) an obvious contradiction between the belief in stringent immigration control and in diversity as contributing ipso facto to social order, but compromise was driven by party-political necessity" (Schain, 2008: 154).

Historically, Britain has been a country of emigration. By contrast with France looking abroad to supplement its labor and army supply or with the US, a nation of nations, Britain did not have a need for immigrant labor. Its needs were fulfilled: two-thirds of those who migrated to Britain before World War II (with restrictions), came through Empire migration with the largest proportion from Ireland. Between 1948 and 1962, there was hardly a rush of immigration from the New Commonwealth countries, Schain observes (2008: 143). Hostile public opinion to the migration of non-whites from the former Empire convinced governmental elites that their policy should contain flows and covertly exclude undesirable subjects. Controls were made easier because Britain is an island and because restrictive administrative check points were efficient in the home countries. After 1991, net arrivals from non-European Union countries almost doubled as outflows of British citizens decreased with a net inflow around 160,000 people. Work permits, family reunification,

DOI: 10.1057/9781137428004.0004

and asylum seeking (which grew rapidly in the 1990s, more than any other European country) explain this situation.

Minority ethnic groups

Such an increase in the number of people from different ethnic backgrounds and countries was one of the most significant changes in Britain at the turn of the 21st century. According to the 2011 census, Britain is still a predominantly white society, with 86% of its population (56 million) from the white majority. Fourteen percent of the population, one in four children under the age of ten in the UK, are from ethnic minorities and account for 80% of the population growth. Ethnicities are increasingly mixed and all groups intermarried. The five largest black and minority ethnic groups (BME) in the UK are Indian (1,412,958 people accounting for 2.5% of the population), Pakistani (1,124,511 people, that is 2% with a 57% increase since 2001), Bangladeshi 447,201 people, 0.8% with a 59% increase), Black Africans (989,628 people, 1.8% of the population, with a 106% increase) and Black Caribbean (594,825 people, that is 1.1% of the population). Minorities are young (25% under 10) and only 5% of them are over 60.

All groups except Indians have unemployment rates that are more than double the rate of the white population according to the Policy exchange report published in May 2014. A co-author of the report, Rishi Sunak emphasizes that ethnic minorities are not one homogeneous political group. They differ in education, employment, housing, trust in the police, and issues affecting their communities.

While minority ethnic populations in inner cities continue to grow, white populations in many of these areas keep declining. Consequently, minority ethnic populations make comprise a greater proportion of the population of some urban neighborhoods in 2010 than they did 10 and 20 years ago.

Still, compared with the US, despite their rapid growth, minority ethnic populations remain small and several other European countries have similar proportions. Currently, the fastest growing group comes from Africa but still comprises only 1% of the population. Populations from the Indian subcontinent form the largest minority groups but their total is less than 5% of the whole.

The concentration of these populations in particular areas is significant. The 37 local authorities (9% of local authorities) with the highest concentrations of all minorities (above 15%) house 61% of the total

DOI: 10.1057/9781137428004.0004

minority ethnic population. Five percent of the local authorities house 38% of minorities (Lupton and Powers, 2004: 19).

Discussion on segregation and the concentration of minority ethnic populations sparks off heated debates about the nature and extent of the problems. We do not have enough knowledge on the impact of segregation on opportunities, mobility, social cohesion and community relations, and consequently, on the way these populations confront threats. It is likely that the concentrations of minority groups in disadvantaged and disinvested inner cities strain service provisions, and increase risks of internal and external clashes, as it has been pointed out by various recent reports after public disorders. It has been shown, nevertheless, that when isolation is reduced and more inter-ethnic relations increased, there is greater acceptance and tolerance among multicultural populations (Lupton and Powers, 2004: 20).

Density remains a controversial issue. For a long time, the consensus has been that population diversity and density in space were assets for cities. However, as remarked by Molotch and McClain (2003: 688), proximity is not necessarily synonymous with social solidarities. Diversity may incite some people (ageing white or affluent communities, for instance) to withdraw from public spaces or control their use. Some may chose to move out. Outward movement of existing populations leaves residual social and economic problems for those who cannot access better locations and their higher costs. This dilemma reveals why the concentration of poverty in inner cities is also linked to discrimination and deprivation. In Britain, social policies supporting multiculturalism limit inequalities but the welfare net has been continuously reduced in the last decade and especially after the subprime crisis of 2008.

Race in Britain

Compared with other Western European countries, the US and Britain share similar patterns regarding immigrant integration and citizenship within common law regimes, and attention to race is a source of division in society (Bulmer and Solomos, 2004; Waters, 2014: 11). Muslims play a more important role in British society than in the case of the US (Peach, 2005). According to some indicators, black Caribbean and Africans appear, indeed, more integrated with whites in Britain than Pakistanis and Bangladeshis. Early on, the emphasis on race and race relations was largely related to concerns of public order. As soon as British society recognized the classification of the population by race and in research, a "race relations industry" developed, leading to anti-discrimination policies in a multiculturalist society, recognized as such. Tools were created such as the Commission on Racial Equality (CRE) launched in 1976, an independent body financed by the Home Office able to conduct investigations to implement equal treatment in the sectors of employment, housing, and education. Thanks to Policy Studies Institute, policemen's modes of policing may be investigated. It helped implement the recommendations made by the MacPherson report. More minorities were hired in police forces through positive discrimination programs. In 2012, the Metropolitan Police Service was 16% ethnic minority, 39% Asian, 28% mixed, 21% Black, and 11% Chinese), a total of 53,000 men (London comprises a 41% non-white population). But the underrepresentation among senior ranks remains at a low percentage of 3% among the 43 local police forces of England and Wales, a force of 129,584 men, 6,537 belong to ethnic minorities, that is, 5% of the total (they were 3.3% in 2004). For Schain however, multiculturalism has been cited as an excuse for not dealing effectively with questions of discrimination. He quotes the head of the CRE in 2004, blaming minorities "for being distracted by tokens of recognition, while being excluded from the real business (such that) the smile of recognition has turned into the rictus grin on the face of institutional racism" (Schain 2009: 158).

Comparing Britain and the US on the topic of minorities, Waters observes that in the latter, the key division is between whites and non-whites or blacks and non-blacks. In other words, on which side, black or white, are Asians and Latinos to be incorporated? In the UK, the distinction is more likely drawn between white British and other BME non-whites (Waters, 2014: 13). Flows of new white immigrants from other parts of Europe (Bulgaria and Romania) and of asylum seekers from beleaguered countries have generated heated debates about the need for restrictive immigration policies. Poles who had come earlier and returned to Poland ten years ago are now settled in the UK and make 12.6% of foreigners (Wihtol de Wenden, 2012: 43). Problems, until recently seen as correlated with "visible" racial minorities (with the exception of the Irish formerly incorporated among the blacks due to their position of exclusion), are now associated with asylum seekers and low-skilled Eastern Europeans. The American concept of "segmented assimilation" facilitates research pertaining on the sectors of society that immigrants and their descendants are joining. The generational differences matter and have been understudied. For Favell, the issue, "related

DOI: 10.1057/9781137428004.0004

systematically back to the political construction of the problem is out of step with the rest of mainland Europe" (2001: 387).

The lack of interest in generational differences is explained by a research focus on social class divisions and mobility in Britain, as was the case for a long time in France. However, since assimilation occurs over several generations, it makes a difference that descendants of Caribbeans in the UK are mostly third and fourth generation, and new groups from Eastern Europe, first generation. Britain does not have affirmative action programs as in the US (it has positive actions) and consequently, it remains to be seen if and how some groups are impacted by an ethnic penalty (Waters, 2014: 17).

Policing the inner city

As the main state institution involved in the provision of social control and order, the police, as a major actor among local authorities, are important, not only for what they are but also for what they symbolize. They are the point of contact between the control apparatus of the state and the citizenry. Crime is an issue that people want something done about, as British Crime surveys continuously confirm. Any electoral campaign pledges anti-crime measures. While the middle classes are largely spared serious crime victimization, they want policy measures in charge of low-level "incivilities." This is not a new story.

In Britain, public disorders were, indeed, widespread all throughout the 19th century. Urban violence was a mode of expression by the masses, deprived of political representation, and a form of violent collective bargaining. At the beginning of the 20th century, however, public and private elites perceived working-class disorders as a threat to their political, social, and economic order; they reacted by criminalizing collective protest on one hand and on the other hand, by praising the virtue of public tranquillity. In the 1820s, the famous remark of Sir R. Peele, the founder of Metropolitan Police Force, that "the police is the public and the public is the police" was characterized by a peaceful form of police intervention which later was interpreted as policing by "consent." In fact, street patrols were highly contested at that time. Strong opposition to the police in a deeply class-divided society forced the police to adopt a low profile with a minimum use of force when intervening in working-class neighborhoods. The lack of brutal repression during working-class demonstrations was, thus, a tactical choice.

DOI: 10.1057/9781137428004.0004

The decline of civil disorder after serious 19th century riots (related to the price of bread, religious strife, and industrialization) could be attributed to the repeal of Combination Acts, which allowed the growth of working-class organizations, the integration of religious minorities, reforming efforts and improvements, the emigration of the poor, the spread of literacy, and better welfare provisions (Anderson, 2011).

Despite persisting socio-economic and cultural inequalities, significant class conflicts came to an end in the 1950s. Bargaining techniques replaced modes of violent face-to-face conflicts and, in working-class neighborhoods, a relative calm accompanied three prosperous decades after World War II.

The first widely publicized and commented incidents were those of Nottingham and of Notting Hill in London in 1958, which immediately were identified by the government as 'race riots'. The violent and complex dimensions of these incidents forced political actors to question perceptions, and accepted ideas about social cohesion and diversity. Hundreds of young whites, with stones and bottles confronted blacks. The political elite, in particular the Labor Party, then in power, warned that a serious "race problem" threatened the country, the solution to which was immigration control.

Why did the government opt to focus on race and immigration? As mentioned before, the construction of race permeates American and British societies and they tie the evolution of racial formations to specific places and specific times.

Other signs of looming social tensions in multicultural cities (for instance, in Leeds en 1972, 1974, 1975) appeared before widely covered incidents in Bristol and Brixton, the latter being the object of a large and well-known report (Scarman, 1985).

France and England have experienced recurrent forms of urban disorder in the last quarter of the 20th century in which police were often perceived as the spark igniting the tinder box. Mobilized actors in recent disorders share the same characteristics: they tend to be young males dressed with indistinct, hooded sweatshirts, living in disadvantaged areas, and reflecting a diversity of cultures. They are generally hostile to institutions and feel rejected.

In the UK, in the 1980s, public attention was caught by young whites confronting Blacks; then the zoom focused on Blacks clashing with the police. In the 1990s, the media reported clashes between young white delinquents acting collectively to confront the police, then in the 2000s

DOI: 10.1057/9781137428004.0004

white "nationalists" confronted young Asians over issues of drug deals in the industrial cities of the North, before multicultural young people ransacked some streets in various British cities during the summer of 2011. We will come back to these disturbances in the following chapter. What is at stake here is the political choice to externalize such youth at a time when economic structuring caused a lot of anxiety among the middle classes. They became scapegoats when society was experiencing deep problems of mutation. Social insecurity boosted civil insecurity; this fed into public knowledge and policing practice. According to Hall (1980: 13), the urban crisis of the 1980s called for police powers to contain and constrain, and in effect, to help criminalize parts of the black population, especially the youth. The "folk devils" of the mugging panic were created by racist discourses fuelled by the race riots taking place in America, seen everywhere in the blogosphere. The succession of Afro-Caribbean criminality was followed by the black activism of the 1960s, to the mugger of the 1970s, to the rioter of the 1980s, and to the ultimate folk devil from the underworld of the Yardies in the 1990s (Keith, 1993: 200–201). Insecurity is one of the few domains left where state authorities can show anxious voters that something can be done to alleviate their fears.

In 1969, Margaret Thatcher was elected on a platform emphasizing a return to order. She recruited police forces, reinforced court structures and stated that "prisons worked." After 1983, more accountability was required from citizens in crime prevention. A professional reactive police, car patrolling problem neighborhoods were perceived as inefficient. New principles of managerialism called for performance and returns after investments, despite budget cuts. The private sector with Crime Concern promoted good practices and multi-partnerships. The voluntary sector with Nacro, the Safe Neighborhood Unit, developed innovative projects, especially in deprived housing estates. Neighborhood watches were encouraged. Twenty cities or so launched safer cities programs (Crawford, 2002: 58).

In 1990–1991, the Morgan report, echoing the Bonnemaison report in France, set the tone for social crime prevention. Preventing crime was a task for the whole community and community safety was preferred to more police-oriented crime prevention (Crawford, 2012: 67). The report encouraged local authorities to work with the police. But the Report's recommendations were not implemented because the central government wanted to keep the upper-hand on such policies.

A new stage, marked by punitive populism, characterized the 1990s. The concept of defensible space (Newman, 1973) called for more specialized

DOI: 10.1057/9781137428004.0004

police units and for the widespread use of CCTVs. According to estimates, in the mid-1990s in England, some 78% of the Home Office's crime prevention budget was spent on CCTS systems alone (Crawford, 2012: 68).

With his catchphrase "tough on crime, tough with the causes of crime," Prime Minister Tony Blair sought to reseize the initiative on law and order. He asked for local authorities' deeper involvement. A *Crime and Disorder Bill* was passed in 1998 (its foundation was a previous 1997 consultation paper from the Home Office called *No More Excuses*). The intention of this bill was to reassure an anxious public opinion prone to fear of crime, by emphasizing its goal of preventing offenses by young people. Police were asked to work jointly with local authorities and develop and promote local community safety partnerships. Multidisciplinary Youth Offending Teams (YOT) were to operate at the local level. Strict sentencing targeted minors (estimated to be responsible for seven million crimes). Social preventative measures intended to bring support to families in crisis. In the short term, community policing and neighborhood watches were promoted, and in the long term, a risk-focused approach (communities that care) was developed.

Another change comes from the use of disorder rather than that of urban violence as in France. The latter term in the 1980s referred to race riots in inner cities where poor black families were concentrated. But the racialized discourse of disorder was challenged by outbreaks involving white youth in public housing estates. "The politics of 'disorder' appears to have lost its overtly racial tone and has taken its place among the mainstream of everyday urban life" Crawford observes (2002: 87). Incivilities, anti-social behaviors became a major theme of crime prevention in the 1990s. A 1998 act on security pursued the goal of preventing low-level repetitive acts of incivility, although the link between disorder and crime was never established, not even by James Wilson, the author with G. Kelling (1982) of the broken windows hypothesis.

Despite the data from the British Crime Survey showing that crime was declining in England in 2004, public perception expressed the belief that crime was on the rise. As pointed out by Garland (1999: 354), two trends co-existed at that time. On one hand, the dedramatization of crime linked to anti-social behaviors and incivilities, and to what he calls "the criminology of the self," and on the other hand, the continuous demonization of cultural scapegoats calling for drastic measures of control and labeled the "criminology of the other." Some incivilities are currently decriminalized and accepted as part of urban life, especially

DOI: 10.1057/9781137428004.0004

in poor areas without public services. Situational crime prevention schemes intend to help communities take the issue of safety in their own hands. Still, the police are given a greater capacity for action when moral, hysterical panics, for instance, about young men and knives, are activated by the media and raise the level of punitiveness of public opinion. In practice, curfew orders, which could be applied for children under ten in specific areas, were not often used (as in France) and eventually, anti-social behavior ordinances also declined: families, more than youths, per se, became the focus of intervention, offering a more all-encompassing lens both for practitioners and local authorities.

To conclude, such shifts in policies raise questions. Heavily criticized, the central government has yielded the upper-hand and more localism has taken over. Citizens who had been asked formerly to leave it to the professionals (as in France) are now enjoined to active participation in a self-policing society (Crawford, 2002: 79). Recent elections for mayors and for police commissioners (met with little success) uphold this view (Loveday, 2011). The culture of performance measurement is heavily criticized at a time when budget cuts impact the police forces. Will they modify police efficiency and trust? The involvement of civil society is supposed to compensate the withdrawal of public services in problem neighborhoods but this also remains a topic of debate.

The US

Historical background

The American Constitution had to impose itself on states' sovereignty and, distrusting the tyranny of power, the Founding Fathers established reciprocal veto powers (*checks and balances*) between the executive, legislative, and judicial branches of power as well as between the different layers of the Federal "marble cake." Rights were given to these branches of power to overlook each other. The US retained archaic Tudorian institutions emphasizing a fusion of functions and a division of powers, at a time when all over Europe and in England as well, adequate tools favoring modernity were tested, implying a centralization of power and a separation of functions. The goal of the Founding Fathers was not efficiency, as Justice Brandheis observed, but the limitation of an arbitrary use of power. For T. Jefferson, the best state was the state that governed the less. Foreigners are often struck by the somewhat powerlessness of

DOI: 10.1057/9781137428004.0004

the American President and a remark by Harry Truman comes to mind: "I sit all day long, trying to convince people to do what it stands to reason they should do without my need to convince them" (Neustadt, 1960: 40). The Presidential institution was not intended to be efficient. Congress was to be the main branch of the Constitution. But as a representative of diversified and rival local interests and submitted to re-election every other year, the House is inefficient and the Senate, when it becomes seized by filibustering is also tied up. Few laws are, thus, passed and inertia prevails.

Unlike the French worshipping of equality, Americans praise most of all the value of liberty. It generates a certain anarchy, the opportunity to get rich without constraints and the right to insurrection within what T. Lowi (1979: 92) called "the automatic society" and others, the principle of *laissez-faire*. Citizenship is not a recurring national debate. Americans' membership is found probably in their adhesion to a bill of constitutional rights and in their identity in a smaller local community. In a federal country such as the US, marked at its foundation by a binary philosophy distinguishing the established and the outsiders, moral insiders are linked by an implicit covenant and by shared values (Elias and Scotson, 1965). A widely spread idea is that only the work of a community upon itself and by itself (*We, the people*) can rescue failing individuals through efforts, deterrence, constraint, charity, and private outreach. The state's intervention must remain marginal and residual. It is not supposed to intervene in social processes which would imply a sort of collectivism running contrary to the ideology of laissez faire (Gallup poll, 2011). Max Weber (1904/1958) refers to the ethic of Protestantism and its determined social selection as the basis of capitalism and of its narration, glorifying winners and ejecting losers (Body-Gendrot, 1993: 16–17).

The representation of interests within two very large political parties also reflects the spirit of the foundations which led to the birth of the American institutional system. That such a vast and heterogeneous nation could put up with only two viable parties shows that they are less the emanation of a central matrix serving an ideology, as is the case in England and France, than of varied forms of coalitions of ill-assorted interests with vaguely formulated goals so that everyone finds a reason for support. That, at the beginning of the 21st century, 35 million Americans would not benefit from a universal health insurance seems puzzling: it is explained by the difficulty of finding a political consensus within a Congress impacted by veto-groups, the goal of which is

DOI: 10.1057/9781137428004.0004

preventing a decision of common interest that would hurt their own particular interests. The free circulation of weapons is another example that comes to mind. According to D. Riesman, these veto-groups play a game of croquet, as in Alice in the Wonderland. For some of them, the state has lost any autonomous power and cannot even play the croquet game.

The idea that all must participate in the solution to a problem is, again, linked to the myth of success. Groups that self-organize efficiently are rewarded by the dominant position they grant themselves. The mode of identity production is meaningful only after sieving, selection, and hier-archization processes have occurred. In each country, criteria are differ-ent. Myths and principles of incorporation are submitted to ruptures, advances, failures, and reappraisal (Body-Gendrot, 1993: 17).

One should remember that the American Nation is an artifact, a crea-tion formed outside of any organic, historical or cultural matrix. Who and in whose name (and not the state which, unlike in France and in England, developed at the same time as the nation) could have inter-fered in the processes of immigrants' self-organization and voluntary concentration? The immigration phenomenon is prior, if not concomi-tant, to the formation of the nation. The mandatory Americanization of European immigrants did take place in the first half of the 20th century, after the American population doubled in size within 44 years, from 50 million in 1880 to 100 million in 1924, compelling national institutions to reorganize, regulate and innovate (Body-Gendrot and Schain, 1982). The principles of freedom and equality were distorted by political neces-sity. At the end of the 19th century, groups hostile to new immigrants from eastern and southern Europe brought into question the inclusive principles that had governed the long period of construction of "a nation by design" (Zoberg, 2006) and the values expressed by T. Paine. The definition of the political community, its limits, acceptable and "accepted" races became a critical issue. No one could become a citizen without the nation's consent (*Elk vs. Wilkins*, 1884). Natives worried that the new immigrants would undermine the institutions and traditions that had made America so successful. They were also worried about losing their jobs. These fears generated a support for a more restrictive immigration policy designed by the Federal state and no more by the states. In 1897, immigrants who were illiterate or sick were excluded. The literary test passed in 1917. Quotas based on the national origin of European immigrants were implemented in 1921 and in 1924, virtually

DOI: 10.1057/9781137428004.0004

ending immigration from Southern and Eastern Europe. After 1924, no state could grant immigrants voting rights.

A nation by design

A nation by design, this is how A. Zolberg (2006) analyzed the American incorporation policy purpose. The laws would not have passed without the support of rural America and the urban intelligentsia. Efforts were made to reconstitute a fictitious nation that never existed, to obliterate the tensions of its creation, and to establish a clear line between the "in-group" and "them." Public schools were a powerful catalyst for Americanization. English was the sole language of instruction in all public and private primary schools in 25 states. "To be a good American included adopting everything from the American way to clean your house and brush your teeth to the Protestant values of self-control and self-reliance" (Schain, 2008: 229).

At the same time, modes of community organization which had enchanted Tocqueville continued to characterize the American social and spatial organization. According to class, national origins, religion, ethnicity, age, sexual preferences Americans made the choice of settling in similar places, they elaborated community rules, elected representatives pledging to defend their identities, their needs and political and ideological choices The origins of the population settlement allowed immigrants to practice their own language and religion and to follow their own tradition as long as their loyalty to America was not questioned. The closing of immigration doors, mobility, mass culture, myth accelerated the phenomenon of immigrants' Americanization into hyphenated Americans. Intermarriage rose from 43% to 73% among third-generation Italians, from 53% to 80% among Poles, and from 76% to 92% among Hungarians (Lieberson and Waters, 1988: 199).

American institutions have oscillated between openness, universalism and the respect of particularisms on one hand, and protectionist local practices and nativist impulses on the other. Humanitarian concerns and economic interests have impacted immigration policies. For Lincoln and Jefferson, civil religion and loyalty to the democratic values were the essential conditions of citizenship. Enduring cultures, religions and morals belonging to the private sphere were, for them, a secondary political matter. Because of numerous factors, including decentralized political parties, immigrants, and their children could develop an ethnic space of their own within the public domain and even appropriate it via

DOI: 10.1057/9781137428004.0004

political "machines" mechanisms. Ethnic groups or racial minorities with the status of American citizens could lobby to defend their interests, the pluralist system frequently would yield to their cultural pressures as long as structural pluralism (separatism) was not at stake. The interaction of disparate cultures has thus given America a unique feature.

Such a model functions on mobility and competition and its counterpart is the exclusion/expulsion of those who are not admitted in the in-group. The American dilemma has not been one of citizenship but of race. It has been to balance the preservation of equal rights and the recognition of racial, ethnic, gender, and age differences to be protected by law.

The ethnicization of minorities

The outcast position of impoverished urban African-Americans creates a singular narrative with no equivalent in other Western countries, not even in those with colonial histories. Through the 19th century, legal slavery guaranteed the US a large, unpaid force identified as racial minorities. After the Emancipation Act of 1863, disgruntled Southerners set Jim Crow laws requiring racial segregation in public facilities and keeping blacks from voting. The result was a widespread disenfranchisement of African-Americans. The color line and conflicts over political and economic rights were the problem of the 20th century in the US Blacks, unable to vote in the South, could not secure the resources needed for education, better jobs and upward mobility. With the industrial expansion of Northern and Midwest cities, their migration began during and World War I when immigrants could not fulfil the needs of the growing economy. The concentration and isolation of minorities in inner cities of the North, their continuous discrimination and prevailing institutional racism laid the foundation for the civil rights movement, meant to eliminate legal segregation and ensure minorities' constitutional rights. Judicial decisions asserted that separate facilities were inherently unequal. Discrimination was outlawed in public and private facilities and voting rights asserted in 1965.

Hence since the 1960s, American institutions have had the difficult task of integrating new pieces into an already complicated mosaic. In a process of ethnicization of minorities, according to Balibar and Wallerstein's formulation (1988: 20), "underrepresented" racial and ethnic minorities have become better incorporated.

For W.J. Wilson (1987), the civil rights movement and affirmative action programs opened opportunities for racial minorities in the 1970s and

DOI: 10.1057/9781137428004.0004

1980s, leading to a declining significance of race. But as the most mobile households left black metropolises, they left behind them a concentration of poor, low-skilled blacks in segregated inner cities. With the transformation of an industrial economy to a service-economy, they were unable to find work. Unemployment, family breakups, poor educational attainment, crime, and addictions characterized African-American ghettos. Such ghettos have their own history, features, and evolution. Immigrants who settled voluntarily in the US were spared such formidable mechanisms of exclusion. The racial order was a founding institution within a stigmatized, constrained, excluded, and relegated space.

D. Massey calls "soft apartheid" such a system (1992) based on a linkage of racialization and criminalization. Due to their strong legacy of prejudice against racial minorities, majorities and their institutions are as much responsible for the ghettos' urban violence as are some of the dominated minorities. During the depression, black households were denied public assistance, veterans military rewards, workers unemployment benefits. In 1940, infant mortality in black families was 70% higher than that of whites, 22 years later, it was 90% higher (Katznelson, 2005). Psychologist K. Clark's landmark study of Harlem pointed out at the dark ghetto's, which have been "erected by the white society, by those who have power, both to confine those who have *no* power and to perpetuate their powerless" (1965: 11). Skolnick remarks that anti-miscegenation laws remained in effect in 13 states until 1968 (1998: 90). White offenders have rarely been punished to the same extent as their black counterparts with white juries systematically discriminating against non-whites. Racial segregation has persisted decade after decade, with steering practices by real estate agents, legal covenants restricting home sales to minorities and poor enforcement of anti-discrimination legislation at the local level. With a system of representation that excludes non-whites from conservative constituencies, the American rule of law has weighed on poor minorities' fates to a degree that is difficult to overstate (Body-Gendrot, 2000: 29).

Affirmative action and the legacy of civil rights' struggles

Affirmative action policies or procedures launched after 1964 attempted to redress the harm that the status of slavery had caused African-Americans in terms of discrimination and segregation, and to give them an equal opportunity of access to education, public housing, and

DOI: 10.1057/9781137428004.0004

employment. Even though at least one-third of African-Americans were able to join the middle classes via the trampoline of affirmative action programs, this strategy has only been partially successful: ghettoized blacks, especially single-parent families, have been bypassed by more recently arrived groups and given welfare as a handout. Yet, many positive changes have occurred to remedy racial discrimination.

As early as 1935, a Federal ordinance imposed fair employment in the public sector. The Truman Administration launched this approach in the army and for firms contracting with the government, but practices never really adjusted to principles. Following the civil rights movement, under the Kennedy and Johnson Administrations, the concept was most of all rhetorical. It was a paradox indeed to deracialize American society while maintaining racial categories to do so. The policy also challenged the principle of merit by granting a preference according to selective features. Inequalities de facto would benefit minority groups with such policy. Obviously, to be successful this policy should have remained dissimulated (Sabbagh, 2003). Politicization got in the way and soon, most groups except white men benefited from such programs, causing a violent backlash.

In the way it counts population, spends public aid, and develops affirmative action programs for minorities, the federal government has produced a three-part classification based on race and has placed in the same categories populations fragmented by class, race and ethnicity. The concerned groups have become aware of the advantage of adopting these classifications for their individual and collective interests. As a result, an official multiethnic society acknowledging multiethnic lobbies and minority coalition-building received legitimacy, while the myth of the melting-pot was being discarded.

The challenges of black activists in the 1960s, impatient with the slow pace following civil rights' victories and resorting to intimidation, forced the political and judicial systems to react, and important anti-discrimination legislation and measures were passed. Minorities obtained better political representation, discrimination was banned in public housing after 1968, bussing programs to better schools in white neighborhoods were launched, hate speeches were forbidden by law, stereotypes were less pronounced in firms with a mix staff and minorities were allowed to have access to legal aid to protect their rights.

There is no doubt that affirmative action programs consolidated the formation of racial minorities' middle classes and their upward mobility. But the structure of power and socio-economic inequalities were not fundamentally alleviated. A more segmented multiethnic and multiracial society revealed the twilight of common dreams. Unexpected outcomes hampered the programs. The recipients of affirmative action programs in universities were frequently suspected of succeeding due to the aid they received, ignoring the basis on their own merit. With the judicialization of immigrant and minorities' rights, a numerical equality of results or a proportional representation displaced what was at the start a moral ideal. Assigned identities and claims led to particularist privileges. Groups became more fragmented by their definitions of differences which soon became more salient than commonalities and less energy was devoted to common bonds and more to the boundaries of distinction. Every group became eager to portray its own victimization, victimhood becoming a catch-all identity. The state actively participated in racial and ethnic clientelist formation and, thus, encouraged this type of lobbying.

Numerous subsequent trials concerning the consideration of race in university admission or to employment lead more conservative Supreme Court Justices to gradually dismantle measures which were initially meant to be temporary.

Policing the inner city in the US

Programs of affirmative action did not address the needs of truly disadvantaged minorities in the inner cities and did not redress the institutional discriminations harming them. Historically, the relationship between police departments and racial minorities has been based on a long series of discrimination, abuse and racial profiling with the police rarely being sanctioned by white majorities. According to a 1968 report by Human Rights Watch, the ratio of blacks vs. whites killed by the police in 14 large cities was six to one. Policemen were implicated in unjustified shootings, serious beatings, deadly blows, and unjustified brutality. The overrepresentation of blacks as victims of police shootings is noteworthy. The ratio of killed black/killed white is in some cities 30 to 1. Between 1976 and 1987, 1,800 blacks were killed by policemen, an over ratio of three to one by comparison with whites. In numerous cases, the victims carried no weapon (Body-Gendrot, 2006: 84).

When more black middle classes reached a more respectable status, they could have expected to be spared by police abuse. But, according to ethnographer E. Anderson, this is not the case, and he tells the story of Shawn, a black student at Yale Law School who was degraded in public

DOI: 10.1057/9781137428004.0004

by the police after neighbors gave them a wrong tip. "There comes a time in the life of every African-American," he comments," when he or she is powerfully reminded of his or her putative place as a black person." They refer to it as "the nigger moment." "The affront very often takes place in a trusted social space or public environment...Emotions flood over the victim as this middle class, cosmopolitan-oriented black person is humiliated and shown that he or she is, before anything else, a racially circumscribed black person after all.... There is no protection, no sanctuary, no escaping from this fact. She is vulnerable" (2011: 253).

Since the 1960s, minorities have mobilized around police brutality issues and racial discriminatory practices. Reforms took place in a number of police departments.

In a surprising move, in 2014, attorney-general, Eric Holder, announced that the Justice Department would pull back from prosecuting low-level drug offenders to avoid harsh mandatory sentences. Prisons are filled with nonviolent offenders who are no risk for society. According to recent data, roughly 80% of young African-Americans can expect to be jailed during their life-time. Forty-nine percent of homicide victims are African-American despite the fact that blacks make up only 13% of the population. Hispanics are less victimized and less arrested but the number of their convictions is growing.

American racial minorities express less confidence than others in institutions such as the military, the police and small business. Only 48% of them trust the police, a 12% gap with whites. Polls show that they do not want less police, but a police force with no racial bias.

Significant progress has been made with minority recruitment and reforms in modes of policing but not all 18,000 police departments of the country are convinced of the efficiency of such changes.

DOI: 10.1057/9781137428004.0004

3
Visible Minorities: Citizenship and Discrimination

Abstract: *For a long time, there has been a strong reluctance to consider police relations with visible populations from inner cities as one of the main causes of urban violence. France has a 30-year history of urban riots, most of them linked to feelings of discrimination in the minds of young contenders of urban conflicts. In Britain, urban disorder opposing police and young men, frequently belonging to minorities, is of low intensity, but hurtful to the localities where they occur. Several types of offenders whose racial profile varies mark recent decades. Their social marginalization and lack of future make them look alike their French and American counterparts. Yet recent disorders in the Greater Paris and the Greater London have distinct characteristics. Criminal violence has replaced civil violence and it may explain the absence of racial riots in the US in the last few decades. The dispersion of poverty and the socioeconomic mobility of minorities contribute to appease social tensions. But, by comparison, no-go areas remain lethal and illustrate the despair of those with no opportunity.*

Body-Gendrot, Sophie and Catherine Wihtol de Wenden. *Policing the Inner City in France, Britain, and the US.* New York: Palgrave Macmillan, 2014. DOI: 10.1057/9781137428004.0005.

An old debate in France

Second and third generations of immigrant origin are a central debate in France. Most of them feel transnational, due to their double citizenship with their countries of origin, to their multiple allegiances (crossed with Islam and the solidarity with the Arab World). But the social origins, perhaps, better explain the violence and contest in the inner cities, as well as the discriminations from which they suffer than their supposed cultural or religious background. The youths of immigrant origin, a group difficult to name and to count is much more diverse than it is presented in the media, linking second generations with urban riots, delinquency and Islamic fundamentalism. Its claims have not much changed since the end of the 1970s because the problems raised have not been solved. The debate on national identity in France in 2010 has contributed to the refocusing on these actors as illegitimate citizens.

The second-generation phenomenon is the result of the French decision to stop the immigrant labor force of salaried workers in July 1974. It has had the unexpected effect of increasing family reunification since then. The second-generation phenomenon began to emerge in the public debate at the end of the 1970s, when the first riots appeared in a Lyons suburb against discrimination by the police and the so-called double peine (double penalty—referring to the judges' decision to deport foreigners condemned and imprisoned to their countries of origin where sometimes they have never lived). This mobilization, along with the freedom of association given to foreigners in October 1981, led to the March for equal rights and against discrimination called the "Marche des beurs" (March of the Arabs), which assembled second generations of Maghrebian origin. They walked from Marseilles to Paris with a triumphal arrival on December 1, 1983. They will be granted the ten year residence card based on the criteria of residence, automatically renewable to some categories of foreigners (foreigners married with French, parents of French children, residents in France for more than 15 years) by a law of August 17, 1984. This step has been considered as one of the most successful results of the associative movement.

Several challenges have put on trial the identity of second generations. First, the disturbances brought on by the first Gulf war (1991) in civic "beur" (Arab) associations question the government about the allegiance of second-generation youths. They have been mastered by the strong associative movement which struggles for loyalty toward the government involved in the Gulf war. Their adherence to Islam has been less relevant than their identification to French citizenship in regard to the expression of loyalty to France within the second generations. Second, the emergence of terrorism. In 1995, Jacques Chirac, the leader of the right at the presidential elections was newly elected as president of the Republic. Under the government led by Alain Juppé, terrorism burst in Paris: two attacks killed travelers on the RER (regional express railway) and the Islamist Khaled Kelkal, who put bombs on the TGV tracks near Lyons, was killed by policemen in 1995.

On May 2002, Jacques Chirac was successfully (86%) elected for the second time to the Presidency of the Republic against Jean-Marie Le Pen. Intense riots arose from the sentiment of police discrimination in the Paris suburbs in November 2005. The actors were second generations of Maghrebian or of sub-Saharan origin. They claimed that they wanted to be treated as French with equal rights and they burned the symbols of republican institutions (schools, kindergartens, gymnasiums) or of racist employers (firms). During the presidential elections of May 2007, Nicolas Sarkozy, newly elected, appointed his friend Brice Hortefeux, Minister of Immigration, Integration, National Identity and Co-Development to develop a strong immigration policy. The title of this ministry, which introduced national identity in immigration affairs, was strongly criticized by intellectuals. The ministry was finally terminated in November 2010.

France hardly recognizes its ethnic components. The Constitutional Council, in November 2007, reached an unfavorable decision regarding ethnic statistics, considering that "All French were born free and equal in rights." In 2008, the Simone Veil report on introducing the word *diversity* in the Constitution also concluded negatively. Another research report held by the demographer François Héran confirmed this trend, limiting ethnic statistics to research uses.

A population difficult to name, to count, and to define

The "second-generation" phenomenon has revealed the settlement of "visible" nationalities in French society: in housing, at school, in local life, in cultural practices, and at work. It was presented as a generation without reference, without an identity, but refusing to take the place of their parents in manual work, and occupying a place as mere citizens. Many stereotypes were assigned to the representation of this population, mostly built around inner cities: violence, drugs, unemployment,

DOI: 10.1057/9781137428004.0005

communities, Islam, ethnic ghettos. Many contradictory trends are blurring the integration processes: identity constructions around religious fundamentalism, victimization from the colonial past, visibility of ethnic belongings and skin color, hyperassimilation to republican values in order to find a place in local public policy and politics. The second generation, which is sometimes the third or the fourth generation, has been successively qualified as the "zero generation," "illegitimate children" (Sayad, 1985), "following generation" (Minces, 1985), or the "generation from foreign origin." It is difficult to define, due to its judicial diversity (some of them are French if they were born in France, others are still foreigners if they were born abroad and came with their parents). Many of them have now acquired dual citizenship due to the extension of "jus soli" facilities in western immigration countries and to the permanence of "jus sanguinis" in Islamic countries of departure (Weil, 2004). The most represented foreign nationalities are people from Algeria and Morocco and recently sub-Saharan countries such as Senegal and Mali. The sons of Portuguese as well as the grandsons of Italians and Spanish, who have become invisible in the French social landscape are rarely defined as "second generation". Self-definitions are also very common and several have been used for the last 30 years: "*beurs*" in the 1980s (from the slang language of inner cities consisting in the reverse of the syllabic order of words:"arab" becomes "rebe" and "beur"), "*potes*" (buddies) referred to the slogan of SOS racism "Touche pas à mon pote" (hands off my buddy), an anti-discrimination symbol, "*jeunes*" to young of Maghreb or sub-Saharan origin refers to the youths of Maghrebian or sub-Saharan origin living in poor, inner cities. In the public and political discourse, the term of "*sauvageons*"(wild young people) with antisocial behaviors has been used by Jean-Pierre Chevènement, a left Home Minister on duty in 1997 to refer to their practices of small delinquency in the streets, and the term "*racaille*" (pejorative term for scum) was used in 2005 by Nicolas Sarkozy, then Home Minister and later president of the Republic, since 2007, alluding to their outlaw behaviors, adding the necessity to "clean the suburbs" ("*zones de non droit*", a no-man's-land) with a strong cleaning product, the "kärcher."

Integration, a deceptive debate

Second generation is often linked with integration: are they integrated? How can we measure their integration? There is a permanent debate about "integration" of the second generations. The term itself has

DOI: 10.1057/9781137428004.0005

significantly varied: from assimilation, used between the 1880s and the 1960s, fitting with the republican model of the social contract with total public adhesion to French values, to insertion, briefly used in the 1970s (a functional approach for short-term workers) and integration, launched in the mid-1970s, but formerly used in Algeria for indigenous populations. Integration refers to "social cohesion," a term used by President Jacques Chirac in 1995 and the political community. The term "community of citizens" was proposed in 1996 by the sociologist Dominique Schnapper (1995). But nobody can define the criteria of integration: who is integrated, comparatively with whom?

Logics of exclusion as a spiral of inequalities and discriminations have been the result of concentration in inner cities built in the 1960s and 1970s for the middle and working-classes, rapidly abandoned by the French, then granted to large families from the Maghreb and sub-Saharan Africa, ghettoized at the margins of big cities. Drug smuggling is the main source of "second-generation" delinquency in France, coupled with urban delinquency (riots with policemen in the streets, neighborhood rubbery). There is a strong discrimination from policemen due to the frequent identity controls in inner cities and public spaces (trains, roads) which often ends in a night in a holding cell (Body-Gendrot and Wihtol de Wenden, 2003).

Several indicators have been suggested to measure integration, but they have also been strongly criticized by scientists arguing that the focus put on origins introduces a level of determinism to the integrationist approach, while other criteria such as social, economic, and cultural background are, perhaps, more important. The 'ghettoization' of some inner cities leads to an accumulation of inequalities where poverty is coupled with ethnicity: the department of Seine Saint Denis (the so-called 93) is the poorest one in metropolitan France and the most "colored" one, in spite of a very active policy of inclusion led by the municipalities. Access to employment is the most crucial discrimination for youths of Arab or black origin, coupled with discrimination practiced by police and administrations. Most "second generations" are culturally integrated even if they are economically excluded. There is also a social promotion of ordinary young boys and girls of foreign and working-class origin attaining middle class status in spite of unemployment and racism. Perhaps the French model of "exception française" is less inclusive for these new French populations than it was in periods of economic growth for Italian, Portuguese, Polish, and Spanish populations.

DOI: 10.1057/9781137428004.0005

The policy responses are a cultural management of collective identities at the local level, delegated to urban mediators of Arab or black origin, showing that the republican model is on the move. A kind of "communitarianism by default" is emerging, via the delegation of responsibilities from top to bottom at the local administrative level. The French experience closely connected, first, with the assimilation approach is now rather called "living together" (vivre ensemble).

Identities and self-exclusion

Political strategies led by "second generations" are hesitating between hyperassimilation for a republican elite aiming at entering a bottom-up approach, and behaviors of dissent (salafist Islam as an alternative way of life, violence on the streets). But anomy is more frequent. Political participation is very low and abstention is high because these new French citizens are young, less educated than many other French nationals, poorly socialized in their families to voting, and feel far from the political debates in spite of an active involvement of elite associative leaders in local life. Some associations have tried to engage the political participation of these new voters, also curtsied by all political parties including the National Front. In most cases, they feel French, the other feelings of belonging being lived at the private and individual levels. But some external factors are very delicate in the internal order, such as the Palestinian question, the first and second Gulf war as well as the Iraq and Afghanistan wars, and they may provoke feelings of open dissent.

Ethnicization of identity is growing in France in relegated districts, along with the rise of feelings of humiliation and escape behaviors. "Visible" populations progressively built constructivist approaches of new identities around local citizenship in the mid-1980s (the "*beurs*"), ethnicity ("Arabs," "blacks") in the 1990s, Islam (the "*brothers*"), and more recently postcolonial specificity (the "*indigenous of the Republic*").

The fight for "dignity" and "respect" is very present in the youth discourse and also expressed in their cultural claims and positions: novels, music, theatre, and films. Ethnicity and postcolonial belonging question republican France, even if the country has been, in the long term, a multicultural one which refuses to accept it. The Berberian language (Amazigh) has been recognized as a language of France. Many young of foreign origin have plural identities, more or less built according to their life experience of exclusion, discrimination, social promotion, and foreign or religious offers (dual citizenship, policy of countries

DOI: 10.1057/9781137428004.0005

of origin toward them and transnational links, religious training). Many girls are torn between several behavioral models. During several football games, some boys expressed their refusal of the French flag or the French national anthem "la Marseillaise" and disqualified them. The adhesion to the Palestinian fight and flag as well as Arab broadcast messages (such as the Qatari one, "Al Jazeera") is very common, expanding potential forms of anti-Semitism and sometimes antiwhite feelings.

But the so-called second generation is also conscious that it represents a market: economic, political, cultural for firms, parties and elections, media—conscious of the necessity to introduce diversity, pluralism, and social openness in their image. Integration (despite its unclear definition) progresses and most "second-generation" members are definitely part of French society, inspiring a young and mixed popular culture, more important than the complacency toward the promotion of emblematic cases of successful stories hiding the majority which merely seeks a simple and ordinary life in France, as French (Brouard and Tiberj, 2005; Arslan, 2011).

The riots that occurred in France in the inner cities surrounding Paris (in the so-called départements "93" and "95") and other large cities in France (Lyons, Toulouse, and Grenoble) spread explosions of violence (Clichy-sous-Bois, 2005; Grenoble, 2010), coupled with some expressions of anti-Semitism, developed on blogs belonging to the association "*Indigènes de la république*" Mouvement of the Indigenous of the Republic (cf. Fofana affair in February 2006: the death of a young French of Jewish culture by a black gang from inner cities around Paris). This situation has to be added to the 70,000 cases of urban violence occurring between January 2005 and 2010, to the many conflicts with policemen in the streets, and to the many youths of Maghrebian and black origin put in detention places and jails.

The crisis is deeply rooted, resulting from the failure of settlement policies for populations of immigrant origin which led to an ethnicization of social exclusion. In the early 1960s, the housing crisis, which lasted since the Second World War, coupled with the massive arrival of immigrants for reconstruction left slums surrounding Paris, Lyons, and Marseilles, in a state of no man's land often called the "zone" (inhabited places around factories).Working-class inner cities were not yet in existence at the margins of Paris and Lyons which are now very multiethnic, but they were more so the result of an absorption of former villages than the expression of ready-made urban projects.

DOI: 10.1057/9781137428004.0005

In 1969, the Prime Minister Jacques Chaban-Delmas decided to get rid of the so-called slums. This led to the construction of high-rise towers in the countryside, far from the city centers, deprived of public transportation because it was the period of the promotion of the individual car. They were inspired from the ideals of the architect Le Corbusier, implemented by many young architects aiming at changing cities in the hope of transforming the behaviors of its inhabitants. A functional approach of the city (there are places to sleep, others to work, and others to go shopping) was preferred to sociability, but without the range of facilities that has been planned (sport and green areas) for financial reasons. The result was bare towers, cut from the access to cities. This massive social housing model (HLM) first sheltered French working-classes who had access to private housing in the 1970s and then, progressively, to large immigrant families who became stuck in these dormitory communities in a context of unemployment due to deindustrialization.

New riots emerged in the early 1990s (namely in the suburbs of Lyons) and many experiments to fight against urban violence were focused on prevention as opposed to repression (the so-called DSQ, Développement social des quartiers). The result was a greater emphasis on places than on individual and family trajectories.

The second utopia was the civic ideal of participation and empowerment of the city by residents involved in collective actions to force them to get involved in their communities. Led by former ideals of local democracy (namely in Grenoble in the mid-1970s), this policy stressed citizenship at the grass roots level, localism to link the population with the territories. Most of the thinkers of urban areas thought that the solution was participation. But nothing was anticipated to help the population (and mostly the youths) leave their cities, have opportunity to attend other schools in Paris or elsewhere to meet other young people, and favor mobility (geographic, cultural, and thus social). The territory of housing determined the mandatory public school, high school, the university at the periphery, and local opportunities to find a job. The local democracy and densification of inner cities was preferred to the opportunity to escape. The progressive decrease of subsidies to civic associations during the 1990s, the general feeling of hopelessness among the youth, the persistence of unemployment, and the degradation of the situation of many families led to despair. Many inner-city youths felt that Paris is another world, not fit for them (cf. the movie La Haine). They never cross the highways separating the *banlieues* projects from the main

DOI: 10.1057/9781137428004.0005

city because they fear other worlds and they are stuck with determinism to the walls of their public housing estate (they are named the "*hittistes*"). No solution has been given to encourage geographic mobility.

Another utopia is the model of the social contract. It supposes a homogenization of the population due to the promotion of citizenship, equality of rights, and secularism but it puts little emphasis on the effectiveness of the implementation of such values on the ground. In August 2005, newspapers such as *Le Monde* asserted that the reason why there was no recent terrorist attack in France, compared with London, was the strength of the integration model which was very cohesive and which succeeded to fight against communitarianism. However, in November 2005, some inner cities burnt namely in the zip code areas delineated "93" (Seine Saint Denis) and "95" (Val d'Oise). The integration question is often set against a context marked by new security questions, actions designed to curb Islamic radicalism and challenges arising from social inequalities. The ordinary integration of the youths of immigrant origin, who leave the working-class condition of their parents thanks to school and university studies, and find middle class jobs and conditions do not meet the interest of most media, such as TV, more fascinated by spectacular social successes, relatively exceptional in nature or by negative heroes or rioters. Most of them are confident in the values of the French ideals of equal rights and citizenship and they feel French primarily, even if they have dual citizenship and a Muslim identity (Bertossi and Wihtol de Wenden, 2007).

But they also think that the French values are not fulfilled because they meet many institutional discriminations in daily life (police, namely, but also justice and prisons); they face unequal treatment at school, housing segregation and employment discrimination; and overall they suffer to be stigmatized as members of an ethnic community when they have struggled to escape from such determinism. All of these assertions are confirmed by the results of research and field studies conducted during recent years. The designation of them as bad citizens worsened their relations with institutions. No answer has been given by the public powers to the request of respect and equality. They do not want to change republican values; they want these values to apply to them. There is no claim for more collective "ethnic" identity, but for more respect and a recognition of their French citizenship in a pluralistic view.

Second-generation youth want to be French but in a nontraditional manner, as demonstrated when some of them exhibited the Palestinian

DOI: 10.1057/9781137428004.0005

flag while supporting Jacques Chirac at the presidential elections of 2002 against Jean-Marie Le Pen. Islam seems to have had no impact during the riots. For the General Direction of the Renseignements généraux (the undercover investigative police): "This was a form of unorganized uprising with the emergence of a leaderless and programless revolt. No manipulation was observed, no action on the part of Islam fundamentalists. The Far Left did not anticipate the outbursts to its great dismay" (2005). It was neither an "insurrection" nor an uprising (Body-Gendrot, 2008). According to the editor of *Le Monde*, J.-M. Colombani (2005), "these were forms of violence, vandalism, the expression of a nihilistic rage, frequently from juvenile offenders. Very specifically, the stage preceding riots; which always have a defined goal, trigger looting, provoke deaths." "The International Crisis Group" (2006, II) confirmed that it is the exhaustion of political Islamism, not its radicalization, that explains much of the violence, and it is the depoliticization of young Muslims, rather than their alleged reversion to a radical kind of communalism, that ought to be cause for worry.

Young blacks were also part of the riots, and half of them were Christians. Some Muslim associations proposed intervention as pacificators to the local mayors during the struggles. Most of the young people were only occasional practitioners of Islam, which explains the success of radical trends to make conversation with those who have a limited knowledge of their own religion. They mostly suffer from the few possibilities offered by school and employment. The more they are segregated, the less tendency they have to move from their localities. Only the most successful have the opportunity to leave their segregated inner cities. Yet a few of them look for an escape in a fundamentalist Islamic way of life.

The geographical area "Seine Saint Denis" (93) where many riots erupt is the poorest "département" (region) in France with many single-parent families with a lot of children, drug businesses, some cases of rape and retaliations of girls considered as too emancipated, expressing their difficulties with men and their will to struggle. A political will to solve the "inner-cities" problem is lacking because richer, nearby localities do not accept social housing units and large families (with social handicaps).

For 30 years, the ritual of demonstrations among the Maghrebian and black youths has used police discrimination as a major bone of contention. Civic associations, theatre teams, "beur" (Arab) novels, and films have been inspired by this strong reality of children and teenagers killed by unpunished policemen or by French neighbors in the end of

DOI: 10.1057/9781137428004.0005

the 1970s. The movements of protest in Lyons and its projects erupted around this topic, claiming equality and respect. It has become a tradition among youths to demonstrate in their inner cities to manifest in their inner cities: protest taking the form of walks, and hunger strikes. The feeling of injustice strongly shared among youths convinces them that they are not treated as French because their differences are easily discernible. The game and the playful dimension have been factors of the extension of violence. The will to give a show to the televisions is also part of the ritual. The youth like to become actors and to be in the limelight. This is a manner to be considered as heroes, even if the prison is at the end of the road.

The riots did not reveal any social movement: no leaders, no slogans, no organizations emerged. It has only been an expression of revolt. In a sense, the existence of riots is a sign of the health of the "second generation" which prefers to appear in public life to express collective disappointment as a game rather than to disappear as such in risk behaviors. Most "second-generation" members did not burn cars, did not participate in riots, or follow an ordinary life of ordinary integration. The sociologist Hugues Lagrange (2008), stressing the social and structural factors of urban riots, analyzes the behaviors of the youth as a mix of resignation and utopia, with an overrepresentation of delinquency mixed with school failure among children of large families from sub-Saharan Africa. The probability of riots is all the weaker as the urban zones are highly segregated and highly policed, with currently few confrontations between various populations. The associations have suffered from being abandoned from the State, although they are considered as essential to rebuild the social link with public institutions.

Britain: youths inner cities and police in inner cities

Few analyses look at how violence erupts in inner cities and with what consequences.[1] Comparative approaches look at structural factors of relative deprivation, social and economic forces at work, at dynamic trends of low intensity, and at their management. The nature, mutations, and dynamics of such disorders reveal variations both within cities and from one country to another during the three decades studied here. Analyzing them allows to grasp how they fit, in a whole set of theories and practices,

DOI: 10.1057/9781137428004.0005

and what continuities or ruptures they introduce. The types of contenders, the sites of unrest, and the different logics from one decade to the other show that they have their own dynamics, according to circumstances, outer forces, and scales of interactions, and that there is hardly any transmission from one generation of contenders to another, even in the same neighborhoods. The diversification of the nature and the forms of disorder generate a reconceptualization of police intervention and of their response to such situations. When disorder occurs, the discretionary power of policemen in the field—what Her Majesty's Inspectorate Constabulary calls "flexible options" in defusing tensions (HMIC, 1999: 59)—cannot be overlooked and it may cause disorders to amplify.

The UK distinguishes *Afro-Caribbeans* (West Indians also called blacks); *Asians* (Pakistanis and Bangladeshis) from the *Chinese* who come in a specific category. (In France and in the US, *Asian* refers to Chinese, Vietnamese, Thai, Cambodians, etc.). In Britain, as in the US, the notion of *community* evokes the cohesion of a neighborhood, to a sense of common belonging which can be ethnic and racial, but not necessarily. It is not so in France, where community refers to either the National Community or the European Community. Communitarianism is fought by majorities, defending the *unus* and social cohesion rather than the *ex pluribus*. Why Britain is characterized abroad as communitarist when everyone is subject to the same laws and has the same rights—though with some exceptions—is debatable.

The "community" is also an administrative tool of management, for instance, in matters of security. Beyond territorial communities, other forms of social bonding and commonalities, in particular social networks, are rapidly spreading.

The types of public disorders (studied here because they caused debates in the media, among the political elites and in public opinion) have little to do with the "riots" experienced in India or China, or even in Los Angeles in 1992. It is not in the number of deaths and massive damages by which they are characterized and the fact that they do not trigger negotiations, as labor conflicts would. The urban violence examined here is a low-intensity form of violence largely covered by the media; it is very disturbing and sometimes devastating for the neighborhoods where it occurs. It should, thus, be taken seriously, as it may be lethal for localities and their neighborhoods' image and reputation. Residents who can, may move out. A stigmatized locality may be deserted by investors, employees, tourists, students, and potential residents. There were

DOI: 10.1057/9781137428004.0005

concerns about the impact of the 2011 disorders at the Olympic Games taking place in the summer of 2012 in London and, to alleviate such worries, organizers were given an added budget, more public forces, and even the army.

The interchangeable use of terms like violence, disorder, outbreak, disturbance intends mostly to refer to a rupture of order. Yet it goes without saying that social order and disorder are deeply intertwined. Several types of protesters clashing with police forces in inner cities have marked the most recent decades without any transmission occurring from one group to another.

The 1980s

The massive arrival of Afro-Caribbeans from the Commonwealth has generated shocks in poor white working-class neighborhoods, disrupting previous arrangements and compromises. They have settled in communities already in decline, where mechanisms of social control, which hitherto had been effective in relatively homogeneous areas, were eroding. Yet, until the first oil shock, the British economy was able to provide jobs and allowed different categories of working-classes to live together without pronounced conflicts.

New forms of violence emanated, in part, from the transformation of the working-class, from the sense of exclusion they felt in an affluent society focused on consumption and social success. The irruption of hooligans in football stadiums at that time (without mentioning the panics caused by the mods and the rockers) has been analyzed by scholars. Rituals, violent modes of operation, and political ideologies occurred in and outside of stadiums. Tribal behaviors (dress code, emblems, songs) and the extreme radicalization of "supporterism" are boosted by a search for peer recognition and the inability of a decaying English working class to transmit traditional socialization to its youth. Hooliganism reveals a malaise, clutching to nationalism (Elias and Dunning, 1986). Campbell (1993), for her part, interprets the aggressive behaviors of such white youths as an overcompensation regarding their marginality, their poverty, and their distrust for conventional norms. Unable to find work in the postindustrial economy, these youths take pride in exacerbated masculinity, in high-risk behavior, in confrontation and continuous challenges to the police. Consequently, any police intervention at the residents' call is a spark that can ignite tension-filled neighborhoods.

DOI: 10.1057/9781137428004.0005

As in other European countries, France in particular, the economic crisis in the 1970s has translated to episodes of violence in social spaces struggling to match the needs of the new economy, a withdrawal of the Welfare state with disastrous effects, and a difficult acculturation of new, young, Muslim generations from the Commonwealth. Successive governments have had to face the frustration of newcomers, stopped by a glass ceiling and by unequal opportunities.

In the early and mid-1980s, recurring confrontations involved second-generation Africo-Caribbean youths and the police. These disorders, also called "race riots" by the government and the media, are illustrated by those of St Paul in Bristol, which are less well-known than those of Brixton, analyzed in the Scarman report. In Bristol, on April 2, 1980, a police raid during a private party at a bar led to the owner's arrest, a well-known African-Caribbean figure (Critcher and Waddington, 1996). The police intervention attracted a hostile crowd and in this highly charged situation, it sparked disorder. The police were assaulted with bricks and bottles for a few hours and had to withdraw, greatly outnumbered by youths and unable to protect themselves. Twenty-three policemen were wounded. For the elites, this incident was a "social aberration" (Benyon and Solomos, 1987). Yet it repeated the following year, in Brixton in April 1981, after a vast police raid called Swamp 81 that consisted of saturating the locality, stopping and searching suspects, and raiding homes to eliminate "muggings." Very serious incidents then took place: 200 people were arrested, 145 buildings were damaged, over 200 vehicles destroyed, and 450 people reported injuries (Waddington, Jobard and King, 2009: 14).

Hundreds of smaller disorders followed: Southall in London, opposing skinheads and Asians; Toxteth in Liverpool and Moss Side in Manchester; Brixton, again, in 1985; Handsworth (Birmingham), Chapeltown (Leeds), Broadwater Farm in London (a policeman stabbed, 233 policemen wounded), Tottenham, Sheffield.

The 1990s

By contrast with the previous decade, the groups of disenfranchised young men clashing with the police in 1991 were white working-class, living in public housing estates in Cardiff, Coventry, Newcastle, and perceived as petty delinquents in areas heavily marked by unemployment. Like youths in Les Minguettes in France in 1981, out of boredom, they were also joyriding with stolen cars, their actions were covered by the media,

DOI: 10.1057/9781137428004.0005

and they confronted the police. Youths "who rarely would move one mile away from their home suddenly became international icons, famous from Toulouse to Tokyo, for a fortnight or so" (Campbell, 1993: 3).

At Oxford, in the area of Meadow Well, car thefts and then arson were routine, until one night in September 1991, after a police chase, two youths killed themselves in a stolen car. Rumors pointed at the police as the cause of their deaths and for four days, the neighborhood was vandalized, set on fire and looted, as Vaulx-en-Velin had been in France in 1990 after a similar lethal chase (Power and Turnstall, 1997).

Then, in June 1995, in the neighborhood of Manningham in Bradford, North of England, two policemen attempted to stop a noisy soccer game taking place on the street and involving a lot of young Asians, marking the entry of a new type of participant. According to rumors, policemen entered a home and brutalized a woman before arresting three youngsters. The area was already a tinderbox and the police, accused of doing nothing to stop prostitution and trafficking (Webster, 2007: 103). The new generation of Pakistanis was less respectful, youths were frustrated by their leaders, accused of making deals with authorities. They organized themselves and were consequently ready to confront racists, criminalizing them in this region. In a mirror effect, each group exacerbated their stereotypes, their intolerance, and their hostility. The police were perceived as inefficient by various official reports.

The 2000s

The disorders that took place in Oldham, Burnley, and Bradford in the spring and summer of 2001 in the UK reflect the antagonisms of two following types of groups: disenfranchised young whites, petty delinquents, some of them close to hooligans, and the far right on the one hand and, on the other hand, young marginalized and resentful Asians. Media coverage of the disorder shaped the context, crystallized extreme emotions, and boosted speculations in each group of whites, Asians, and the overwhelmingly white local police. The outbreaks of Oldham, in May, involved 500 people; police officers were wounded and the damage estimated at £1.4 million. In Bradford, in July, the same number of people participated, 326 policemen were injured, and the damage amounted to £10 million. The Burnley disorders analyzed below have been documented by the Denham (2001) and Cantle (2001) reports and ended up with recommendations.

DOI: 10.1057/9781137428004.0005

The Burnley disorders

Burnley is a locality of 91,000 residents. In June, rumors of imminent attacks of racist whites mobilized young Asians. Burnley is an immigrant neighborhood representing about 5,000 people, 5% of the population, concentrated in three public housing estates which are 60% Pakistani. During the elections of 2001, the National Front won 11% of the ballots. The usual scenario—tensions, ascent, climax and decrease—was predictable in a conflict-ridden context. Numerous fights over drug trafficking involved, indeed, either white or Asian drunk youths. Pakistani cab drivers regularly complained of racist harassment and one of them was assaulted with a hammer by whites and died. The inadequate police communication heightened tensions. Angry Asians armed themselves with knives and baseball bats, and confronted drunk whites hurling racial injuries. After three nights filled with tension, calm progressively returned.

2011

At the beginning of August, after a peaceful demonstration following the death of a West Indian, Mark Duggan, by the police in Tottenham, a poor neighborhood north of London, outbreaks took place two evenings later and rapidly attained other areas. Tottenham is a multi-ethnic neighborhood. That the August disorders kicked off in an iconic site in London—Broadwater farm, where a police officer was killed in 1985—was a key event for the police as well as the community. In 2011, diverse motivations pushed heterogeneous individuals and groups to act out in grief and anger after the death of a well-known figure in the community, hostility to the police, as well as the opportunity to experience a "happening," the thrill of playing hide and seek with law enforcers, or the opportunity to commit arson and to loot stores.

What was new was the use of Blackberry's encrypted instant message service and other social networks by hooded and masked youths heading speedily to the designated areas. The police were ill-equipped to monitor such services. On the first night, youths resorted to their usual repertoire: police cars were burnt, stores looted, and several buildings set on fire. On the following night, two officers were hit by a speeding car and disorders continued. Then, outbreaks reached Hackney, various London neighborhoods, and Birmingham. The murder of a 26-year-old took place in Croydon, south of London. Because the disturbances kicked

DOI: 10.1057/9781137428004.0005

off in a different way on the third day (spreading to other parts of the country as well as across London), the police were able to "protect" some sites in London (Oxford Street, Westfield shopping centers for instance) but local high streets felt the brunt of the disorder (Clapham Junction, Croydon, Ealing, Hackney).

The fourth night, about 700 people were arrested in London and 100 in the center of Manchester. Leeds and Liverpool experienced similar unrest. Damages were estimated over 200 million pounds. The seriousness of the damages is explained by another trigger which operated during these chaotic four nights: older individuals, a minority of them gangs, made use of the disruption of order, and instrumentalized the violence for their personal benefit. They orchestrated the looting with efficiency, intending to sell back their stolen goods with profit. Three Pakistanis in Birmingham were run over and killed trying to defend their stores. Five people died during the unrest. What the participants had in common, it seems, was an unfocused hostility, a detachment from their communities that allowed them to act spontaneously (also possibly boosted by the consumption of alcohol).

Regarding the police, the response was slow and inappropriate on the first night (the family of Mark Duggan was not personally informed of his death by the police and filed a complaint). At first, strategic errors were made. Once in control with backup arriving from nearby regions (overall the whole 16,000 officers were on the streets of London four days after the start of the outbreaks) and the courts' active support, the police arrested around 4,000 individuals and 2,420 of them were charged with a number of offences (Metropolitan Police, 2012), while the courts' tough approach (two-thirds were sentenced to between 10 and 16 weeks of imprisonment or transferred to high courts, 9 out of 10 arrestees had previous criminal records) (Singh et al., 2012: 29) was overtly supported by the public. Governmental measures of zero tolerance advocated the suppression of family benefits and the eviction of delinquent families from public housing units. Political parties in opposition (including former Prime Minister Tony Blair) and human rights groups criticized such a punitive posture: toughness would not hide the consequences of a lack of welfare services in deprived inner cities.

Comparing English and French disorders

In another work (Body-Gendrot, 2013), these events have been compared with those taking place in France in 2005. They reveal convergences:

DOI: 10.1057/9781137428004.0005

urban outbreaks take place in urban areas carrying multiple indications of deprivation, sheltering populations of diverse cultural origins but with different trajectories of mobility. In such areas, the police/population relations are frequently tense and marked by distrust. Youths, who are heavily unemployed or still in school, have no hopes and no future. For the first time in decades, the disorders in Britain were not qualified as "race riots."

Major features also distinguish them. Firstly, the length of disruptive actions, which lasted three weeks in France in 2005, marks a difference with the three days of disorder in England. Secondly, the stages for action were not similar: 300 neighborhoods in France were disrupted and just those in a few cities in the UK. Wealthy Paris was guarded like a medieval fortress with two ring roads protecting the city from the poorer revolted projects, while the boundaries in London between affluent and more impoverished neighborhoods were less sharply delineated. Mixed public housing estates are spread all over the city, including at the core. Beleaguered youths could not march to Paris and the railway stations were under heavy police surveillance. Thirdly, looting in England was a manner for young people, older than in France, to grasp something, anything. Little or no looting was reported in France where frequently, the teenagers' goal was to confront the police and settle the score with institutions like schools which had excluded them. Fourthly, social networks played an active part in England, indicating empty streets with no police surveillance and giving the demonstrators the power to assemble, to plan, to share. This was less the case in France where cell phones were used mostly to check whether the media made the youths' actions visible.

Fifthly, extensive British television coverage was devoted to victims and to their emotions during the 2011 events. Calls for denunciation by authorities and methods helping citizens to do so via images caught by CCTVs were, then, enforced, while self-help and innovative collective actions intending to repair damages were praised. This trend supporting victims and blaming the looters' "sick culture" is rarely supported by the media in France and when President Sarkozy, responding to the anxiety of an inner-city resident, expressed his will to get rid of the "scum" (juvenile delinquents), he was heavily criticized. Blaming the police for causing social tensions, due to their lack of accountability, their methods of harassment, and their disrespect for their "clients" is routine in France, where youth whose lives are chaotic, parents overwhelmed, education dysfunctional, are rarely pointed at as "shaming" the nation.

DOI: 10.1057/9781137428004.0005

A culture of "excuse" prevails in this Roman Catholic country. Juvenile court judges write editorials to support such culture. Nevertheless, in France, this "compassion" does not generate more public mobilizations of solidarity with the inner-city projects among majorities. The British residents' spontaneous attitude of self-help, their expression of solidarity with victims, and the organization of collective actions are reminiscent of that of New Yorkers rushing to Ground Zero to help after 9/11. Although there seems to be growing incivility in sections of British society, declining civility, and increasing noncooperation with the police, surprisingly high levels of interpersonal trust distinguish British culture from that of the French (Body-Gendrot, 2013).

Regarding police reforms, in Britain in the early 1980s, following the Scarman report, urban unrest had a positive effect on policing and on race relations, and more antidiscrimination measures were implemented. A similar observation was made after the MacPherson report. But in 2011, new measures, such as reductions in the number of police officers and the election of police chiefs, after being temporarily halted by the House of Lords, were enforced. By contrast, in France, the police is the "strong arm of the state" due to its centralization and its political instrumentalization. One can even speak of an overinvestment of policy-makers in their attempt to secure sensitive areas marked by large public housing projects, leading to paramilitary modes of policing and a saturation of space by law enforcers, in some cases. Conversely, disenfranchised youths in France often instrumentalize disorder to intimidate local politicians and obtain what they would not get otherwise (summer camps for their younger brothers and sisters, public jobs, etc.). Allocation processes, then, rely more on bargaining processes and on tests of strength, than on multiculturalist policies as in England (Jobard, 2008: 239–240).

Cycles of unrest are also linked, in France, to recent migration patterns, for instance from sub-Saharan countries, with very large families isolated in disinvested enclaves, as mentioned earlier. Some populations are unable to articulate their demands except, now and then, violently.

Repetitive disorders since the 1990s appear to have led nowhere, and there has been no significant difference of approach between left and right governments in response to such events. Policies meant to buy social peace remain incremental and inefficient to improve the residents' social mobility. However, the capacity of French residents of deprived neighborhoods to establish their grievances on political agendas via collective violence is proven by the amount of subsidies they receive from the state.

DOI: 10.1057/9781137428004.0005

The US: a strange lull

The absence of racial riots in the US in more than two decades can be partly explained by the internal differentiation which occurred among African-Americans in the last 20 years, by a better incorporation of minority middle classes in the mainstream leading to their geographical dispersal, and the rightward orientation of the country strengthening the punishment and incarceration of the "undeserving" poor.

However, the path taken to reach the reduction of racial tensions has been long and strenuous.

The evolution of the law and order issue

The mobilization of the American middle classes on the law and order issue was deliberately launched in the 1960s by conservative political entrepreneurs.[2] Before that time, families would leave the doors of their homes open; children would play on the street and walk home from school without supervision. But during the 1960s, American urban dwellers became alarmed by their unsafe streets. There was more property crime in late modernity societies: due to affluence and more consumption, more goods were left without surveillance and therefore, became a target for petty thieves (Garland, 2001). Burglaries and thefts increased. Violent crime against persons also increased, as internal mechanisms of neighborhood control and protection were decreasing. Many households comprised two wage-earners, leaving their homes empty for most of the day. Although the FBI statistics are to be taken cautiously, they indicate that the rate of property crime rose by 73% in seven years. Violent crime doubled in the country between 1960 and 1969. Conservative politicians—Wallace, Goldwater and later Nixon—eager to find a cementing theme, used the elusive issue of law and order to address "the forgotten American." They amalgamated fears about racial riots, anticonformist student demonstrations, and rising urban crime into a powerful denunciation of the "soft" liberal state. They played on representations, and on the insecurity caused by major changes occurring in American society and based on racist stereotypes, creating a spontaneous link—a form of racial code—between black crime and white victims. Their strategy was successful.

In 1964, at the beginning of a series of bloody summers, a memorandum written by the Department of Justice for President Johnson and entitled *Riots and crime in the 1960s* anticipated the kind of political exploitation that this context of unrest could lead to. Street crime was a real

DOI: 10.1057/9781137428004.0005

threat for many, it said, not a political smokescreen. Demographically, the number of young men was increasing at a faster rate than the general population and anticrime programs had to be strengthened. It advocated the creation of a Crime Commission. The President's Commission on Law Enforcement and the Administration of Justice issued a report in 1967 called *The Change of Crime in a Free Society* along the same lines. At the end of the summer after very serious race riots caused deaths and casualties, especially in Detroit and Newark, the president addressed the nation and urged it to "attack...the conditions that breed despair and violence...ignorance, discrimination, slums, poverty, disease, not enough jobs...not because we are frightened by conflict, but because we are fired by conscience.... There is simply no other way to achieve a decent and orderly society in America." In 1968, the U.S. Riot Commission produced the famous *Report of the National Advisory Commission on Civil Disorders*, better known as "The Kerner Report." Then, in 1969, Milton Eisenhower, the president of the U.S. National Commission on the Causes and Prevention of Violence, handed the president *To Establish Justice, to Insure Domestic Tranquility: Final Report.* Most of these reports linked patterns of crime and violence to structural changes occurring in American society such as the age distribution, the increasing number of minorities living in large cities, the lack of mobility for number of their youths, cultural transformations, and mutations in the criminal justice system. In other words, they pointed at urban life as conducive to crime. But the changes they recommended were at such astronomical costs, at the time the US was waging a war in Vietnam that they were unlikely to be implemented.

The Johnson Administration made the mistake of announcing a "War on Crime," linked to the "War on Poverty." Not only is it difficult to establish a link between reducing poverty and reducing crime, but crime can never be eliminated, despite a presidential pledge. Moreover, such announcements assigned too much importance to the issue and allowed the conservative opposition to play on fears. Their advertisements would show, for example, a white woman walking a dark and deserted street, while a voice gave statistics on crime. Yet, the possibility for a woman being raped by a stranger was as likely, then, as that of being hit by lightning. America was much safer in terms of murders than in the 1930s, before the end of Prohibition (the murder rate had decreased by 50% in 1964) (Flamm, 2005). Fear, however, was real in cities.

DOI: 10.1057/9781137428004.0005

Because the protection of women and children was frequently portrayed against a black mugger, and although race and crime were not identical, in conservatives' campaigns, they overlapped. In 1967, riots became the first issue of concern for Americans worrying about their personal protection. Law and order was the decisive factor in R. Nixon's narrow triumph. The context of riots destabilized the Johnson Administration ("each riot costs me 90 000 votes," the president said) (Flamm, 2005: 37). He was blamed for pushing his Great Society and social prevention programs as an adequate solution to civil unrest.

The debates around the law *Safer Streets* passed in 1968, indicated that Congress, controlled by Democrats, had also attempted to take hold of the issue of law and order, which, until then, was a prerogative of states, counties, and local governments. This law provided additional resources from the Federal government to local police forces and to prison managers on the basis of successful results. FBI eavesdropping was legally allowed by law in order to stop subversive suspects (meaning Black Panthers or Martin Luther King for instance), with or without a judge's warrant. Weapons' sales were to be more controlled. Intuitively, L.B. Johnson understood that the issue of civil disorder and crime could cost him the elections, even if B. Goldwater's campaign on such a theme in 1964 was premature. The federalization of the crime issue started, then.

As a consequence of these political maneuvers, in the last quarter of the 20th century, a new civil and political order developed in the US, based on crime and on the fear of crime. The precautionary principle, a powerful ferment for a binary order, unified Americans around their refusal to become the victims of crimes. "We are crime victims. We are the loved ones of crime victims. Above all, we are those who live in fear that we or those we care for will be victimized by crime" (Simon, 2007: 75, 109). (Victimization surveys launched by N. Katzenbach started in 1965 and were then given visibility by the media.) A "culture of fear" and an imaginary centered on potential victimization, erased differences among people, and led them to support punitive forms of populism against alleged or real troublemakers. Judges (elected or appointed) found themselves under attack for their neutrality, competence, and judgment. Prosecutors became the champions of victims and of the alleged general community interests (Simon, 2007: 33). The extension of the definition of crime and the growth in punishment led prosecutors to play a prominent role. A less democratic, more racially polarized and

DOI: 10.1057/9781137428004.0005

more uncertain America took shape, Simon observes (2007). The arsenal of security measures that proliferated henceforth did not make cities more secure. It fed an endless quest for zero risk.

From this moment on, there were choices regarding where to live, work, send children to school: choices were made according to the perceptions of risk and to the representation of "Dangerous Others." The "Exile project" is twofold, Simon observes. It is a "constellation of commitments that presents Americans with the option of obtaining more security for its beleaguered urban cores only by sending the young men of those communities into 'exile'" (Simon, 2007: 143). He examines the evolution and growth of American prisons in this process of exile to rural areas. Between 1990 and 1999, a prison opened in rural American towns every 15 days. "Locking out" mirrors the "locking in" asylum process, that is the choice that middle class Americans made of isolating themselves in gated or secure communities, a process which reinforces that of prison and benefits the administration, the security market, and political authorities. Order and regulation replaced the idealized solidarity of the New Deal and fed the citizens' "alienation and rage." Many citizens seemed to opt out of politics and to fight for their self-interest, ignoring collective commitments. A legitimacy is, thus, given to the development of high technologies of surveillance, to SUV's with reinforced bumpers, to barriers enclosing properties, and to other ways of distancing oneself from others, thus reinforcing distrust (except inside of the security bubble). As, in the later part of the 20th century, fears were given more visibility by the media, an almost "siege mentality" grasped heavy television viewers. "The sheer number of frights, exaggerated or not, takes a toll, making it easier to view each succeeding problem as a mortal danger based on the emotions one remembers from the last one-enhanced further, perhaps, by what one's parents conveyed about the one before that. Far from being inexperienced with threats, many Americans may be suffering from threat fatigue" (Stearns, 2006: 195).

When 9/11 occurred, Americans were already accustomed to the jeopardy of their freedoms for safety purposes. In one generation, mentalities had interiorized suppression, and zero risk had become a sensible expectation, if not a right. Property defense allowed all kinds of populist abuses. The revolution, which occurred then, was not that of more punishment and less reinsertion for delinquents but "the moulding of citizens spurred by fear and conformism" (Simon, 2007: 39).

DOI: 10.1057/9781137428004.0005

In the 1990s, while violent crime declined with the end of the crack epidemics, among other reasons, the issue was kept on the political agenda, in the media, and among the city residents' concerns. Less public space became available, more identity checks and more surveillance were employed in less hospitable cities.

Don't American cities burn any longer? Sometimes, they do

Inequalities kept growing since 1973, poverty increased, the unemployment rates remained high, if one includes those who have stopped looking for work, police brutality still generates high frustrations (American police kill around 400 people a year, most often in a situation of legitimate defense) (Bonnet and Thery, 2014). So one wonders why, except for Miami in 1989, Los Angeles riots in 1992, Cincinnati in 2001, and Ferguson in 2014, American cities no longer experience no widespread disturbances as in the 1960s.

Historian Michael Katz (2012) has led a comparison of factors provoking disorders in the French and American political and ideological contexts. For him, the relative absence of (collective) urban violence is explained by a new ecology of power which we will document below (whites and blacks do not live in the same areas), a selective incorporation of minorities in the labor, education, and housing market and in the local power structure and by the mass consumption society. He acknowledges that the assumption that young African-Americans are depoliticized should be checked. Significant research validates infrapolitical mobilizations/demonstrations (Scott, 1990). Looking at American migrants' mobilizations, mostly Latinos, in 2006, Katz explains that these demonstrators trust political institutions and rely on them to grasp more rights and equal treatment, a major difference with urban violence in France. Provided with jobs, they detain a legitimacy which allows them to request Federal intervention to be protected, for instance, from local police abuse. By contrast, the attitude of visible minorities in France appears closer to that of excluded blacks, he says. This is partially true. What Katz ignores is that the young men who participated in the disorders in 2005 were mostly French teenagers, but with very diverse origins, a major difference with the Latino or black participants that he examines. Over two-thirds of the delinquent juveniles in France are located in the Greater Paris and they involve several thousands of young people. They are not structured in gangs as in Los Angeles and they are not divided by race and ethnicity as is the case in American cities, but they are groups

DOI: 10.1057/9781137428004.0005

of idle youngsters between 13 and 25 years whose identity identifies with the place where they live and make a living out of various traffics. They live in what might be called a counterworld, with few adults around. A minority of them (estimated between 5% and 10%) are responsible for numerous street crimes; they guard their own turf and attack those who do not belong to their neighborhoods. Firemen are attacked along with postmen, teachers, social workers, bus drivers, not to mention doctors, delivery people, and storekeepers in what looks like no-go areas. This has led to the abandonment of whole areas, where police forces are reluctant to go (Body-Gendrot and Savitch, 2012).

Immigrants in America do not have the weight of colonialism in their imaginary, as these poor immigrant children do. Moreover, the term "immigrant" is too large and does not take into account origins, generations, gender, time, and place revealing very diverse trajectories. Katz's optimism relative to immigrants in America is questioned by the defederalization of immigration policies now left to the states and by the xenophobia of some local legislatures (i.e., Arizona), by immigrants' economic exploitation and the cultural deterioration of numerous first generations. He does not take into account the role of the generous French welfare state (politique de ville) buying peace by providing numerous jobs to kids from poor neighborhoods and access to better schools. He only focuses on disenfranchised youths (estimated to 5–10% per locality).

Katz (2012: 79) acknowledges that, if widespread civil violence—burning, looting, sniping at the police—no longer characterizes American cities, nevertheless criminal violence keeps plaguing these cities. Poverty-ridden areas where frustrated men turn their rage inward or against others remain extremely dangerous. There, drive-by shooting, gang warfare, and violence translate into homicide rates six or seven times higher than in Europe (Nelken, 2010). Collective massacres in schools, or in public spaces keep questioning a culture unable to restrict the circulation of 300,000 million guns causing 32,000 people to die each year (Nocera, 2014) and to take care of dysfunctional individuals.

Katz is right in pointing out that criminal violence has replaced civil violence in the US. The Trayvon Martin case did not generate massive destructions or violence. Protests remained limited to the city of Sanford, Florida. G. Zimmerman, the murderer of this young black, pleaded self-defense and in the county of Seminole in Florida, where blacks are only 12% of the population, the popular jury made of Latina women found

DOI: 10.1057/9781137428004.0005

him innocent. Numerous explanations have been offered to this puzzling verdict and to the absence of mass reaction. First, the "Castle" doctrine allows citizens in Florida to take the law into their own hands and shoot if they perceive a possible aggression to them or their property. Second, in the post-9/11 society, Latinos have become the first minority, bypassing blacks. Third, it is more difficult for large advocacy organizations in the black community to mobilize excluded blacks when the incident does not involve the police of a large city. Fourth, large cities' police have learned how to communicate with minority leaders and to quell anger, after the police shot a minority member. Negotiations take place, judges from state or federal courts may impose police reforms as was the case in New York, Cincinnati, or Los Angeles. In Sanford, Florida, the police chief was fired after the Trayvon Davis case and the new police chief, a black, recruited more minorities. Seven policemen were fired. The new policing approach has narrowed links with minority communities.

A less segregated society?

In the last 20 years, according to the 1990 census, blacks had moved from central cities to the suburbs; 56% of those who identified themselves as both white and black lived in the suburbs, expressing different suburbanization patterns than single-race identifiers who remained in central cities. The share of whites living in the suburbs (73%) was in decline, while the share of blacks who lived in the suburbs (39%) was growing (Frey, 1990). Table 3.1 shows the growth of the metropolitan areas since 1980, the stability of the suburbs (sprawl started again in 2012), and the decline of nonmetropolitan areas.

M. Berube (2011), a research director at the Brookings Institute, commenting on the state of metropolitan areas from the 2010 census pointed out that racial and ethnic minorities accounted for an astonishing

TABLE 3.1   *Metropolitan location of Americans*

	1980	1990	2000	2010
Metro area (%)	74.8	77.5	79	80.7
Nonmetropolitan area (%)	25.2	22.5	21	19.3
Central city (in numbers)	80,149,076	87,484,629	95,974,320	101,620,459
Suburb (in numbers)	94,945,446	116,762,873	137,118,311	156,697,304

Source: Bureau of the Census. We are grateful to John R. Logan, Professor of Sociology, Director, Spatial Structures in the Social Sciences, Brown University, for updating these data.

DOI: 10.1057/9781137428004.0005

91% of US population growth in the 2000s. Hispanics and Asians alone accounted for almost three-quarters of that growth. The combined population of cities in the 100 largest metro areas is now fully 59% nonwhite. Their suburbs are more than one-third nonwhite. They are home to a majority of metropolitan blacks. Blacks' 51% suburban share is up from 44% in 2000 and 37% in 1990 (Frey, 2011b: 9). This is the first time that more than half of every major racial and ethnic group in major metro areas lives in the suburbs.

One of the explanations is that a mixture of policy changes like 'Fair housing' laws and subsidies for low-income homeownership, combined with the aging of suburban infrastructure, has made suburban housing more accommodating of racial and ethnic diversity. Nearly half of all voucher holders, and more than half of all rental units priced below Fair Market Rents, are located in the suburbs (Berube, 2011), as will be seen with the case of Ferguson, MO. The past few years may be accelerating further economic diversification of suburbs, which in regions like Chicago and Detroit, are the primary locus for foreclosed homes. Chicago, for example, is now about one-third white, one-third black, and one-third Hispanic (Frey, 2011b).

While the suburban poor do tend to live in less poor neighborhoods than their city counterparts, the prevalence of high-poverty suburban communities—where more than 20% of people live below the poverty line—expanded rapidly in the 2000s, as illustrated again by Ferguson, MO. Over time, this may introduce more suburbs to the myriad challenges associated with concentrated poverty, including poor-performing schools, private-sector disinvestment, health, crime, and safety issues.

In view of such contrasting data offered by the Census and Brookings reports (Frey 2011a and 2011b), the question is whether the progress experienced by African-Americans has remained resistant to change and how does this group compare with the new immigrants in terms of discrimination?

A slow improvement for racial minorities?

In the last 50 years, a reduction of frictions and the lowering of discrimination for women and blacks have translated in wage increases (57% for black women vs. 39% for white women and 33% for black men vs. a lowering of 4.3% for white men, according to the National Bureau of Economic Research in 2012). However, gains in income and wealth made

DOI: 10.1057/9781137428004.0005

during these decades have been shattered by the economic downturn which has followed the end of the subprime crisis. After the bursting of the housing market bubble in 2006, nine million households had their homes foreclosed and a brutal housing crisis lasted ten years. Moreover, as one in five middle class blacks hold jobs in the public sector, they felt particularly threatened by layoffs as a strategy to address the fiscal crisis in numerous cities. Jobless unemployment rates among black Americans have consistently been about double those of white. In 2012, it was 15.1% compared with 8% for whites.

The expelling of low-income workers and the unemployed from government social welfare and health programs as well as from corporate insurance and unemployment benefits hit particularly those at the bottom, mostly minorities (Sassen, 2014: 1). A series of screens filter minorities into more or less promising statuses, progressively dividing them along lines full of implications for their economic futures (Katz, 2012: 49).

A study from the Pew Research Center analyzing data from the US Census (July 26, 2011) reveals that the median wealth of white households is 20 times that of black households and 18 times that of Hispanic households. Wealth gaps rose to record highs between whites, blacks, and Hispanics. From 2005 to 2009, due to the subprime crisis, wealth fell by 66% among Hispanic households and 53% among black households, compared with just 16% among white households. A third of blacks (35%) and Hispanics (31%) had zero or negative net worth in 2009, compared with 15% of white households, a marked growth in poverty since 2005. In 2008, only 18% of blacks and Latinos had savings accounts compared with 43.4% of white (Ehrenreich and Muhammad, 2009). Within each group, those in the top 10% had their share of wealth rise during those years.

In brief, the transformation and the restructuring of the American economy and the ascendance and domination of finance at the turn of the 21st century have only benefited a small percentage of the population. Such inequality can be described as a kind of expulsion of numerous social categories from the well-being they should have earned through their labor (Sassen, 2014: 15).

The events that took place in Ferguson, MO, in August 2014 indicate that American cities or at least their suburbs may burn, after all. Why did this city of 21,000 north of St Louis experience ten nights of unrest over the fatal shooting of an African-American teenager, Michael Brown, by white police officer Darren Wilson? The results of state and federal investigations will elucidate the circumstances of that death and the local police accountability. They will clarify whether the police officer acted in self-defense, and the militarization of the white local police, using weapons of war and pointing rifles at black protesters has to be changed. But at the time of this writing, the trends developed above regarding race and poverty shed light on the context in which this death took place.

A "fateful decision" of the city of St Louis in 1876 led it to separate itself from the county (Smith, 2014). In most of the US, after 1920, suburbs grew twice as fast as city centers. Most cities of the Rust Belt, St Louis, was plagued by entrenched poverty after jobs and the white middle class left the center for affluent suburbs of a county fragmented in 90 municipalities. Ferguson was a largely white suburban enclave, 85% white, as recently as 1980 (Kneebone, 2014). Then many poor black households from the northern part of the city moved out to better suburban neighborhoods. According to the 2010 census, Ferguson's black population reached 67%, and the city's unemployment rose. Its poor population doubled and roughly 25% of its residents live below the poverty threshold ($23,500 for a family of four) (Kneebone, 2014). Consequently, the quality of city's services (education, health, the police) has declined.

The recent arrival of blacks in Ferguson in the last 15 years has not allowed them to create powerful defense organizations and become part of the power structure. The city remains virtually all-white: a white mayor, a white City Council except for one black, a white school board with only one Hispanic, a white police force except for 3 blacks out of 56 members (Smith, 2014). Will there be more minority representation after the Ferguson's rioters requiring justice? It is doubtful. The time of affirmative action programs is over. The lack of residents' participation is also striking. In the last municipal election, only 6% of blacks voted. The turnout for whites was 17% (Smith, 2014). The tensions between the poor black population and the city's authorities come partly from blacks' exclusion from economic and political arrangements. Unlike in St Louis, the local police's involvement with the community has been minimal (Hunt, 2014). The police's revenue relies disproportionately on traffic citation revenue (DWB, driving while black); blacks are pulled over, cited, and arrested in numbers far exceeding their population share, according to a recent report from Missouri's attorney general. If they cannot pay the fine, they are sent to jail. Last year in Ferguson, 86% of stops, 92% of searches, and 93% of arrests were of black people—although police

DOI: 10.1057/9781137428004.0005

officers were far less likely to find contraband on black drivers (22% vs. 34% whites) (Smith, 2014). If the fines cannot be paid, the offender is sent to jail and may lose his or her work. No wonder then that when police use violence against stigmatized minorities, especially when police kill minority youths with impunity, it sends a message to a community that their lives are not valued and the state does not represent them. If there are no alternative paths to pursue justice, riots are likely. No feature of a racially divided society represents racial domination or instills the message of subjugation more forcefully than police. Therefore, riots are the last resort for those who find all other paths to justice blocked, C. Schneider observes (2014). One can add that the absence of conversation between black population leaders (including church leaders) and the white decision-makers in Ferguson also explains why the upper levels of authority including President Obama and Attorney General E. Holder, both black, along with the National Guard, had to intervene. Some observers (Bonnet and Thery, 2014) detect a new type of riots with the Ferguson case. As documented by Janowitz (1979: 263–265), communal racial riots in 1910–1950 over contested urban territories denounced a color line segregating blacks in northeast cities; then, commodity riots within black communities were outbursts against property and retail establishments plus looting. In Ferguson, thousands of demonstrators supported by black national organizations' leaders, this time denounced racial profiling, and the white police's fatal shootings of American blacks, frequently unarmed, each year in numerous cities; they also expressed outrage at the police's disrespect (Michael Brown's body lay in the open, exposed in public view for four hours under a heavy sun); they point at the "overmilitarization" of poorly trained local police forces in suburban America. But, as observed by Hunt (2014), the racial divide remains, captured by a Pew Research Center survey on the handling of M. Brown's death: 65% of blacks said the police response went too far, only 33% of whites agreed; 18% of blacks expressed confidence in the investigation that will be led both at the state and federal levels. Although the local police's behavior was questionable—withholding the name of the officer who shot M. Brown, confronting demonstrators with a show of force and armored cars with snipers on top—the claim of the police officer that he acted in self-defense will be defended by his lawyers. As many as 300 million weapons are esteemed to circulate in the US. Recent decisions from the US Supreme Court (*Plumhoff v. Rickard* in 2014 and *Comnick v. Thompson* in 2011) make it extremely difficult, if not impossible, to

DOI: 10.1057/9781137428004.0005

convict policemen and the local authorities employing them in case of civil rights violation and power abuse. But should more fatal shootings occur—"in 2012, according to the FBI, American police officers shot and killed 409 people. Their British counterpart shot and killed no one. The Japanese have killed one in the past six years" (*The Economist*, August 23, 2014: 11)—if there are no policemen condemned, more disorders may occur.

Notes

1   This part borrows from Body-Gendrot (2012: 124 and sq).
2   This part borrows in part from Body-Gendrot (2013: 42–46). Copyright Routledge.

DOI: 10.1057/9781137428004.0005

4
Policing the Inner Cities

Abstract: *Inner cities where police/community relations are marked by distrust have experienced disorders usually followed by police reforms. In Paris, although, in railway stations, the police have been shown by researchers to stop and search minorities more than others, based on their appearance, discrimination has remained a taboo. In London, such issue remains a source of tensions and the police may be taken to court. In New York, a court found the police guilty of "indirect racial profiling." Are Muslims a suspect category for the police? It is claimed that neighborhoods are searched because there is suspicion of troublemaking or of potential plots. Is community policing the adequate approach for the police? It may be so in decentralized countries.*

Body-Gendrot, Sophie and Catherine Wihtol de Wenden. *Policing the Inner City in France, Britain, and the US.* New York: Palgrave Macmillan, 2014. DOI: 10.1057/9781137428004.0006.

Police–community relationships are frequently characterized by distrust and suspicion in disadvantaged, minority neighborhoods where disorders, more than order, conservatively defined, prevail. Police officers know "the shops, stores, warehouses, restaurants, hotels, schools, playgrounds and other public places in such a way they can recognize at a glance whether what is going on within them is within the range of normalcy" (Bittner 1974: 90). But making police work efficient either for preventative or repressive actions takes a long time and numerous practices do not reach the desired results. The lack of legitimacy of the police in the eyes of a majority of residents feeling overpoliced and underprotected may, then, limit the efficiency of police work.

In the US, as analyzed by Braga and Weisburd (2010: 40), during the 1970s, researchers attempted to find out how effective police strategies were in inner cities. Discouraged, they reached the famous conclusion: "What works?" As David Bayley stated, "the Police do not prevent crime. This is one of the best-kept secrets of modern life. Experts know it, the police know it, but the public does not know it...the primary strategies adopted by the modern police have been shown to have little or no effect on crime" (1994: 3). Augmenting police cars, equipment, and patrols in problem neighborhoods, giving rapid responses to emergency calls, changing patrol strategies or differential intensities of surveillance, strengthening military discipline and structure in the police organization, launching "wars on crime," and so on, do not bring residents an improved feeling of security and trust in the police (Gottfredson and Hirshi, 1990: 270).

Moreover, in poor minority neighborhoods, abrasive relationships between police and residents remain a major source of grievance, tension, and even violence. Before its composition changed with a new black police commissioner, to many black residents in many American cities, the white police force seemingly acted unfairly, like an occupying army, rather than as a public service paid with taxpayers' money.

Consequently, in the 1990s and 2000s, there was a general consensus that police practices had to be reformed. Without relying on solid research, innovative police programs and practices were launched in various cities, a decentralized approach since the American police are comprised of 18,000 local forces, that is, 13,000 municipal forces, 3,000 sheriffs, and on the whole, one million people (730,000 policemen). They focused on problem-solving in risk areas, hot spot policing, territorial securitization, or means of searching for suspects following principles

DOI: 10.1057/9781137428004.0006

of *new management*. Technological innovation following such principles, such as the statistical tool Compstat, contributed to help police forces implement these strategies. Compstat combines a crime-mapping instrument with management of the police forces in order to preserve important resources and use them instead for selected targets. In New York, according to official figures, after two years of this method, felonies were down 25%, murders down 39%, auto theft down 35%, robberies down by a third, and burglaries down by a quarter (Bratton and Kobler, 1998: 154).

The Britain and France also experienced reforms and innovation and the police chiefs were asked by political authorities to adjust their approaches in order to adapt to residents' expectations. But as will be shown later, they were not easily implemented, especially in a centralized country like France with its top-down model of organization, where too frequently, the police are caught between political injunctions and the reluctance of constables to continuously implement reforms lacking coherence. Moreover, controversial issues such as identity checks and racial/ethnic profiling never leave the agenda. They are still currently a topic of research in the three countries.

Policing hot spots

While France, in the 1980s, relied on social prevention, on the strengthening of social ties, and on delinquents' social reinsertion in problem neighborhoods within a comprehensive urban policy called *politique de la ville*, pragmatically, common law countries opted for crime prevention. Rather than reform the offenders, the idea inspired by Newman's defensible spaces (1973) was to harden targets, protect potential victims, and reduce opportunities for crime on microterritories. Such a strategy of crime prevention led to the "hot spot" approach for policing (what the French call *zones sensibles de sécurité* and currently priority zones): more police resources are allocated to clusters of places, street segments, and public housing estates that are the loci of numerous incidents. Crime maps and geocoding are used by the police staff to avoid dispersing their resources and focus on targets.

Experiments of preventative patrols in Kansas City had yielded impressive results in crime reduction in the 1970s (Sherman and Weisburd, 1995). However, many police chiefs in the US were not convinced. In the

1990s, the new strategies that were tried, adjusted to much smaller territories that were easier to control. The underlying conditions, situations, and dynamics of delinquency were transformed by a whole set of urban policies, not just police strategies, implying poverty dispersion, massive public housing destruction, and the use of technologies of surveillance in at-risk areas. Problem-oriented policing worked to identify why things went wrong and to frame tailor-made responses with multidimensional tools for specific communities under principles of new management. In some cities, outcomes were spectacular but in others, multidimensional problems prevailed and residents complained about police saturation.

During these decades, the UK and France also struggled with security in their inner cities, the problems of which were increased by general contexts of economic insecurity and by flows of poor immigrants and asylum-seekers moving in deprived communities and replacing those who had moved out. Restoring safety in the public space of one place frequently implied a displacement of problems to another location. Basic police tools remained limited in the three countries. Identity checks was one of them.

Identity checks

Stop and search is frequently the first "police-initiated" contact that citizens have with a police officer (Skogan, 2004). Millions of stops are carried out every year. For Sherman (1997), they are one of the few policing tactics that works. But not everyone agrees. Who is stopped and searched predominantly by the police? Is the approach efficient? Is it fair? Young men, many of them members of visible minorities, denounce racial/ethnic profiling. The European Commission against Racism and Intolerance (ECRI, 2007: 39) defines racial profiling as "the use by the police with no objective and reasonable justification, of grounds such as race, colour, language, religion, nationality or national or ethnic origin in control, surveillance, or investigation activities." Policemen conducting stops and searches in the inner city are frequently accused of abuse, harassment, and discrimination by those who are controlled and that the police call by their name. Stops and searches representing specific moments of interactions between the former and the latter under the eyes of closely knit communities, frequently single-parent households, are sources of tension. So does the media coverage of stops and searches

DOI: 10.1057/9781137428004.0006

triggering serious disorders, for instance, when police intervene during peaceful block parties made of old and new generations, and endanger young children, senior citizens, or make use of flash-ball and tear-gas and harm individuals. If amateurs are then present with their cell phones or video equipment, they may be able to provide proof of police aggressive behaviors.

How do the three countries deal with this controversial issue? France ignores ethnic and racial statistics and the Republican principle presumes an equal treatment for all, but some policemen are denounced all the same by defenders of human rights for their discriminatory practices. The UK and the US acknowledge minority constitutional rights and if institutional racism comes to light, antidiscrimination policies and sanctions are enforced. But this does not imply that reforms looking sound on paper will be fairly implemented and enforced. The Courts may be asked to intervene.

French experiences

Former research on identity checks in France

Identity checks are a widespread practice of social control. Law enforcement officers in France are frequently accused of carrying them out in sensitive neighborhoods on the basis of physical profiling (*contrôles au faciès*), which are discriminatory practices. But to show that there is a pattern of discrimination, it is not enough to prove that police stop and search certain groups more than others. First of all, as elsewhere in Europe, the police must prove that they have a reasonable suspicion to do so and secondly, these groups are disproportionately targeted in relation to the population present in the relevant geographical area.

Former studies of identity checks conducted in France were based on self-reports by those previously stopped, collected in monographs or opinion polls. They revealed the resentment of those who were stopped. But such claims were subjective and scientifically hard to verify.

That the French police would betray forms of racism was demonstrated in research by Wieviorka and his colleagues (1992: 262–267), conducting an investigation among police officers participating in discussions with trained researchers, by Monjardet and Gorgeon who studied the evolution of attitudes among cohorts of policemen, observed how they shifted and acquired an in-group mentality of "us" and "them," over ten years

DOI: 10.1057/9781137428004.0006

(2005). Levy (1987) brought the proof in his field study that there was more acute repression, if offenders were North Africans. Duprez and Pinet (2001) revealed the strength of prejudice during oral police recruitment examinations leading male North Africans to fail more often than others. Jobard (2003b) examined the willingness of police officers to file complaints and require compensations when those accused of rebellion or outrage were North Africans or blacks. The police have "clients" and based on their suspicion they exert an acute surveillance of them (Body-Gendrot, 2009).

That judges are reluctant to condemn policemen, the strong arm of the state, for their misconduct or acts of discrimination is not specifically French. However, unique to France is both a tendency not to intervene to redress institutional discrimination or to promote minorities' constitutional rights. For victims and their families, the judicial process may seem extremely long. It sometimes takes several years and gives them the feeling that the police are above the law. Policemen's testimonies are taken under oath. Most of the time, the case is closed or dismissed, for lack of proof. Also on the side of the police are the judges' privileging of the policemen's telling of their story, the support automatically brought to them by their counsels or their lawyers, and the ability of the police or judge to denouncing the plaintiff for obstruction or contempt. According to the French Criminal Code, contempt is punished by a six-month prison term and a 7,500€ fine. It consists in "any words, gestures or threats...addressed to persons discharging a public service mission, acting in the discharge or on the occasion of their office, and liable to undermine their dignity or the respect owed to the office that they hold." (art. 433–435). Obstruction is defined as opposing a person holding public authority (art. 433–436 of the Criminal Code). It receives the same punishment as contempt. The third offence is assault on an officer, and it is a misdemeanor. Such denunciations of claimants by policemen may occur even before the plaintiff is heard by the judge. All these elements give policemen the last word and discourage citizens from going to court against policemen (Jobard, 2003b).

A European comparative survey on identity checks

A vast population survey was carried out in 2008 by the European Union Agency on a sample of 23,500 immigrants and ethnic minorities in the 27 member states. An additional 5,000 residents from the mainstream populations of ten EU countries were also polled, usually from urban

DOI: 10.1057/9781137428004.0006

areas with concentrations of foreign populations. The goal was to study how police forces conducted their searches and whether doing so, they revealed possible discrimination.

Paris, Marseille, and Lyon and their inner cities were selected in France with same-size samples of North African, sub-Saharan Africans and mainstream populations. Respondents indicated their ethnic identity (FRA 2009). It appears from this study that police searches were more frequent in France than in any other of the nine countries: 38% of North Africans, 46% sub-Saharan Africans, and 21% mainstream respondents reported having been searched, revealing a particularly intrusive way of policing populations. While 65% of the mainstream group reported having been treated respectfully, only 44% of North Africans and 27% of sub-Saharan Africans agreed. This finding matched the high distrust expressed by the latter toward the police. Another specificity of France has to do with preemptive identity checks, when there is no breach of law and regardless of the target's behavior. The law stipulated that some-one must always be able to prove one's identity and foreign nationals are required at all times to carry proof of their right to be in France. But how are the police to know that they are foreigners? According to the Higher Court assertion (Cour de cassation, April 25, 1985), the presumption needs to be founded on "objective elements deduced from circumstances external to the person of the interested party," which is a rather vague formulation. An individual cannot contest the legality of such police action since police officers do not have to justify what they do. If an individual refuses to be checked, and is taken to the police station, only then will there be a written report on such identity checks.

The survey of 2007–2008 in Paris

Researchers F. Jobard, R. Levy, J. Lambeth, and S. Névanen (2012) resorted to a rather complex methodology to report how identity checks were carried out by the French national police. What follows are the broad lines of their account. The Soros Foundation-sponsored study of French police profiling in Paris illustrates, indeed, the difficulty in isolat-ing ethnicity as an element in police profiling and in checking whether the latter is ethnically biased in France. The Parisian study was broadly inspired by a similar experiment carried out in Russia. The first tasks were to choose the observation sites, select and define the variables of the study, train monitors, write a questionnaire for subsequent interviews of some of those who had been stopped. Five locations within two railway stations, Gare du Nord and Châtelet in Paris were chosen. There had to be sufficient police activity to allow the monitors to operate without being seen and enough light to see what was going on.

Gare du Nord was selected because it is the largest railway station in France and one of Europe's busiest. The Thalys rail service connects it with Belgium, the UK, and the Netherlands and it has its own law enforcement corps. It connects with dozens of metro, and with peripheric, national, and international lines. Each year, more than 180 million people go through Gare du Nord.

Châtelet-les-Halles was the second selection. It is also one of the busiest subway station in Paris, with 36 million passengers each year and connections between the periphery and the core of Paris.

As for the variables, the *perceived* ethnicity, relating to appearance and visibility of those stopped and to police perceptions, was what had to be recorded. Stereotypes held by policemen were to be taken into account by the researchers including categories as "white," "Arab," "black," "Indo-Pakistani," and "Asian" as well as age, sex, clothing, and the absence or presence of bags (due to terrorist risks). In the police file card recorded by the police database in France, 12 "types" are applied: white, Mediterranean, gypsy, middle-eastern, Maghreb/North African, Eurasian Asian, Amerindian, Indian, Mixed race/Mulatto, black, Polynesian, Kanak-Melanesian. For five months, the monitors observed and recorded how police checked identities. They would either just check someone and ask one or two questions, or stop and frisk, or stop and search bags or pockets, or stop and detain individuals. Some of the people stopped were subsequently interviewed responding to a questionnaire and the coded answers were, then, sent to Soros to be analyzed instantaneously. The benchmark population differed from one location to the other. For example, 86% of the Thalys population was white and 3% Arab, while whites were only 43% and Arabs 15% at the Gare du Nord regional train station (RER).

The major results showed that people dressed in "youth culture" streetwear made up 47% of 525 stops, but only 10% of the benchmark population. Arabs were 7.6 times and blacks six times more likely to be stopped than people of European appearance; out of those two minority groups, two-thirds were dressed in "youth culture"-style. Researchers Levy and Jobard point out that clothing is a racialized variable. In all of the locations, youth urban clothing was a significant risk factor for all the groups formed on the basis of apparent ethnicity. In most cases, a young white male without a bag was seven times more likely to be stopped

DOI: 10.1057/9781137428004.0006

when wearing youth urban clothing. Blacks formed 43% of the sample and only 14.5% of them wore youth culture clothes—urban streetwear. But this minority of a minority was almost always stopped. Only 3% of those stopped complained of racist or disrespectful treatment by French police officers, according to the report.

It is difficult to determine the exact influence of race and style of clothing on French police action. At one location, Arabs were almost always stopped but in other locations, there were no difference between blacks and whites if they wore youth streetwear: they would be stopped. Another major result of this study is that location matters and has an influence on the probability of being stopped. But each location has its specific characteristics, ruling out an all-encompassing analysis of the phenomenon, researchers remark. The central role of location is to be correlated with ethnicity, sex, age, bags, and clothing.

Whereas this study is opening a new path in a country known for ignoring ethnicity is not known, the researchers emphasize its limitations, however. The selected railways were those with large crowds and where police activity was high and consequently, unnoticed. It is likely that within public housing projects, the checks carried out by police officers would stir up feelings of discrimination, due to the concentration of "visible" minorities in such locations. The individual characteristics of the police officers on patrol, specifically those belonging to ethnic minorities, are also missing in the study. Does the police force composition influence their behavior and how are their actions perceived by those with whom they interact? What instructions were they given? These questions, the researchers acknowledge, need to be explored further (Jobard et al., 2012).

Since 2014, police officers in France have to wear a seven-digit number on their uniform allowing identification. The police unions (but not the gendarmes) have expressed their discontent, claiming that police officers were outrageously suspected of racial profiling. Their strength has allowed them so far to refuse delivering a ticket after a stop, and the carrying of a portable camera, as it is already done in some European countries. The number on police uniforms, aiming at ensuring transparency in police actions, also intends to tighten the links between the population and the police.

French police and racism

A national poll from the French Institute of Public Opinion (IFOP) in November 2013 indicates that only 14% of the French think that the

DOI: 10.1057/9781137428004.0006

police are close to the population. Are they meant to be? And what is meant by population? Very few French have contacts with the police.

Two ethnographic pieces of research with diverging views have been recently analyzed by Gauthier (2012), himself a police researcher. These pieces of works summarize what their experience was like when they spent time with police patrols in problem neighborhoods and what views on the issue of police racism they got from these experiences. Jobard (2008) was one of them and for him, if there is racism in police forces, it comes from practicing their job in delinquent areas. Racism functions as a specific autonomous category. In other words, it is less individuals' or groups' ethnicity or race which is at stake for the police than their belonging to risk categories. But for the other researcher, Fassin (2013), racism plays a major, radical, and militant role in discriminatory police practices. Searches are repetitive and unjustified, they are brutal and humiliating. Words have a predictive value and frequently, behaviors are coherent with them. Racism is tolerated by the police hierarchy and police "act white" in sensitive neighborhoods, like a colonial army. Gauthier (2011), for his part, has not met such situations. From his experiences in France and in Germany, he examines how the issue of racism is seen by the policemen from the two countries. First, the racist policeman is always "the other." Second, police officers distinguish various forms and types of racism among their colleagues. There is a generation gap between older policemen in France who have been impacted by the Algerian war on the one hand and on the other hand, a better educated, younger generation of policemen. According to the latter, older policemen, socialized in the police at the end of the 1950s, reflect a culture and modes of thinking despising Arabs, communists, and intellectuals. However, they are fewer and fewer nowadays, compared with more "open," tolerant, and younger policemen. Frustrations from daily job practices, unmet expectations, and a continuous interaction with delinquents belonging to visible minorities reinforce stereotypes nurtured by a background of disenchantment. "In all my professional life, I have never registered a complaint by an old Turkish woman who would have been assaulted. Strange, right? It keeps you thinking. They are also in the public space but nothing ever happens to them, or very rarely," a 55-year-old German policeman remarks (Gauthier, 2012: 8).

Our own interviews confirm Gauthier's views: once policemen become aware that they are less tolerant, they can easily blow a fuse and become utterly pessimistic about the judicial system (releasing young

DOI: 10.1057/9781137428004.0006

delinquents too easily), about politics manipulating the police institution for electoral gains, and about society in general not paying enough respect to their work, they ask to be transferred, for instance, to more bureaucratic positions. In sum, what may appear as racism in the police may come less from racial antagonisms than from routine frustrations (Body-Gendrot, 2009).

French institutional frame to struggle against racism

In France, however, several laws have tried to fill the gap with other European countries. The first one against racism in France was adopted in 1972. Then, following the European directive of 2000, the law of November 16, 2001 punished racial discrimination in the access to social and economic life and the law of December 2002 reinforced penal sanctions when the facts were accompanied by words, writings, or behaviors directed toward a person due to his religious or ethnic belonging. Some notions such as indirect discrimination have also been introduced. It does not directly harm victims but it has secondary consequences on victimization of some categories of people. Progressively, ethnic discrimination has been outlawed. But practices did not follow suit. In 2002, Jacques Chirac, newly reelected, tried to give a new impulse to the integration model, from the fight against discriminations to the "Egalité des chances," or positive discrimination. An independent authority, the HALDE (Haute Autorité de Lutte contre les discriminations et pour l'Egalité), was created in 2004. The arrival of Nicolas Sarkozy at the Presidency of the Republic in 2007 introduced a new evolution, mixing positive discrimination topics and the stigmatization of young people from inner cities (discourse of Grenoble of July 2011 and on the "foreigner" in his Discours of Villepinte during the presidential campaign of May 2012). But the introduction of quantitative targets for prefectures namely for repatriations led to many misleading practices. Justice rarely severely condemned police behaviors in proportion of the grievances perceived by the population. In April 2011, the Appeal Court of Paris temporarily put an end to the Clichy-sous-Bois affair, which led to the riots of 2005, adopting a nonconviction classified decision ("non lieu") in favor of the policemen. At the time of this writing, more judicial decisions are expected.

As for the border controls in April 2011, the Court of Justice of the European Union considered that being undocumented was not a penal fault, which prevented authorities from holding them in custody. Since January 2013, the undocumented can be brought to a police station for

DOI: 10.1057/9781137428004.0006

identity check for a period which cannot exceed 16 hours. This administrative restraint of 16 hours has replaced the former custody period which lasted 48 hours maximum, a situation leading to many breaches of the deontology of security. But the practice does not always fit the goals: many associations, lawyers, and judges consider that the places of retention are places of discretionary outlawed justice practices. In July 2013, for the first time, the Tribunal of Paris attacked the French State for ethnic profiling: 13 victims of identity checks considered that they had been the subjects of random checks because of their skin color. The State replied that the checks were discriminatory, but that the policemen had the right to do it. Many observers are debating about discretionary behaviors in police practices, namely those of the street crime unit BAC (brigades anti-criminalité Anti-Crime Brigade), operating in urban areas, viewed as an elite corps but often pushing the limits of legal rules. Many local associations were stressing that point, such as in Calais and Dunkerque, where the police harassment against undocumented migrants hanging around in the streets before trying to cross the Channel to the United Kingdom is obvious, while others, like Human Rights Watch, are still focusing their reports on the humiliating identity controls.

However, President François Hollande, in his presidential campaign, exposed his will to fight against ethnic profiling. The climate has improved between migrants and policemen in some places. The Defender of Rights Dominique Baudis, who replaced the Police Appeals Commission and the High Authority of fights against discrimination and for equality (HALDE) in 2011, also complained about the use of flash-balls by policemen and required a stricter practice of identity checks in his reports of December 2012 and 2013, with a ticket given by the policeman to the person checked. This procedure was rejected by the Home Minister, M. Valls who considered it as too heavy to manage daily. The policemen were reluctant to accept a stronger management of identity checks set up to improve the identification of the suspects and the control of security frisks. Giving a ticket to the checked person has been abandoned. In its report of November 2013, the National Council of Cities (Conseil national des Villes) stressed the feeling of fear from the population of so-called sensitive districts and of the policemen themselves, the preference put on punishment over protection, the lack of accessibility of police offices, the distrust between police and population, the failures of the development of a police of proximity. Among the

DOI: 10.1057/9781137428004.0006

critics, centralization, quantitative targets, the refusal of the special role of policemen within the population are mostly mentioned.

In its report of 2013, the CNCDH (Commission Nationale Consultative des Droits de l'Homme—National Consultative Commission on Human Rights) points at the freedom of expression regarding the hate of the other, "as if the racist, anti-Semitic and xenophobic ideology was always here." The report includes contributions of all ministries to the fight against racism and discrimination. The Home Ministry insists on the role of its agents fighting against ordinary racism in the streets along with the LICRA (League contre le racisme et l'antisémitisme—International League Against racism and Anti-Semitism). On identity checks, its action has consisted in adopting a new code of ethics on January 1, 2014 for police and gendarmerie recalling the rights and duties in the respect of human rights: exemplarity toward the population, training on racial discrimination at all levels of the hierarchy, support to victims of racism, protection of religious places of worship, against anti-Semitic and anti-Muslim attacks, improvement of the management, ethics of responsibility, an identification number worn by policemen, a yearly cartography of identity controls, use of portable cameras by the police in high risk urban zones, an improvement of practices in Prefectures for the delivery of residence cards.

Some lessons seem to have been learnt from the past decades, but the topic of police discriminations has not been dealt with as a central issue. The policemen, according to the Defender of Rights Report in October 2012, are reluctant to employ a stronger management of identity checks set up to improve the identification of those stopped and the stops-and-searches practices.

British experiences

Former research on police identity checks

The Scarman report

Racial riots erupting in the 1980s and the 1990s in England were subsequently analyzed by the Commissions of investigation that were summoned by higher institutions or by the government. Widely circulated reports were published, loaded with recommendations. One of the most notorious ones was the report written by Lord Scarman (1985) at the

DOI: 10.1057/9781137428004.0006

request of the conservative Home secretary after the racial disorders of 1981 in Brixton, a Greater London neighborhood. It pointed out complex political, social, and economic situations marked by structural inequalities, making minorities' conditions of living (including high unemployment, poor quality of housing and of education, economic deprivation, and a lack of amenities) much worse than for whites. It stipulated that racial inequality was a daily reality in Britain and an important cause for the Brixton disorders. "We must react rapidly, Lord Scarman wrote, if we do not want it to become an endemic evil which would threaten the very survival of our society" (1985, title 9.1).

The media coverage of disorders also played a role in their extension. But for Lord Scarman, the spark to the tinder, in that Brixton environment came from modes of heavy policing, and from a hostile police force. This assumption was confirmed by David Smith: "the riots in 1981 and 1985 were fundamentally anti-police riots" (Smith, 1987: 69). Stops and searches frustrated and exasperated those who were submitted to them without seeing a clear motive that would justify police action. Endless harassment, insults, and persecutions gave young blacks the feeling that local authorities did not care. The report pointed at the arrogance, the brutality, and verbal violence of police officers interacting with racial minorities. Lord Scarman did not write that the police displayed "institutional racism" but he admitted that some police practices are involuntarily discriminatory. Grievances expressed by minorities were rarely taken into account by the police. Lord Scarman pointed at a loss of trust in the police from many minority members. He mentioned that the imperative to enforce the law would sometimes be incompatible with the imperative to maintain the peace. The relationship youths have with the police would deteriorate so much that they become "hostile and vindictive" (Scarman, 1985, title 4.1).

In summary, Lord Scarman wondered how public tranquility could be restored for marginalized populations and suggested that antidiscriminatory approaches would improve minorities' social insertion. To alleviate the resentment felt by young blacks feeling brutally abused, the report recommended a hiring and training of a more ethnically and racially diverse police force, the recruitment of mediators required to consult the residents, the dismissal of rigid procedures, and more flexibility toward change within the institution. He emphasized the hiring and the training of culturally diverse police officers (1985: 125).

The influence of the Scarman report is noteworthy. It was followed by a number of police reforms. In the areas with concentrations of minority

DOI: 10.1057/9781137428004.0006

populations, efforts were made to recruit a police workforce with a profile matching that of the residents. If such goal was partly reached, the promotion of black policemen remained slower than for others. Training courses on race awareness were introduced and fair treatment of all by the police urged. Then professional standards of conduct and the goal of servicing the population were buttressed. Sir Paul Condon, the new Commissioner of the Met, stated that "we must be equally intolerant with our own colleagues who fail to reach the required standards...We have a moral duty to the communities we serve, not only in the way we serve them, but also in the way we conduct our own affairs. How will the public expect us to treat them if we cannot even treat each other fairly?" (*Independent* February 2, 1993).

Nonetheless, it remained difficult in practice for the Met to become a color-blind institution. Significant levels of prejudice which had been observed within certain police forces in the post-Scarman period prevailed in the post-MacPherson one (Rowe 2007). For that reason, due to an inability by the institution to promote racial equality inside its ranks, the first Black Police Association (BPA) was created in 1993–1994.

The MacPherson report

The next most influential report in terms of police reforms, the MacPherson report, was issued at the end of the 1990s. It made references to the Scarman report and remarked that reforms suggested by Scarman had been too narrowly implemented. On the whole, inertia had prevailed, because, as suggested by D. Smith, "it is easy to talk about reforming police forces...to be rather sententious about standards of police conduct.... It is *much more difficult actually to change what really happens on the ground*" (Smith, 1987: 74).

The MacPherson report investigated the murder of Stephen Lawrence, an 18-year-old of Jamaican origin, by white teenagers in the white Eltham neighborhood, southeast of London in April 1983. The indifference and inaction of the local patrol of the Metropolitan police service triggered a debate that stirred public opinion, but not right away. Numerous witnesses had testified to the police on behalf of Lawrence as the murderers were well known and close to the National front; they did not hide their racist views. But only inertia had prevailed, no arrests followed the murder and no information had been given to the family. It took the latter five years to turn their son's death into a *cause célèbre* (famous case), after three botched police investigations, the intervention of the

DOI: 10.1057/9781137428004.0006

Queen's prosecutor, and one more year of counterinvestigation which led nowhere. The family's lawyers eventually turned to the coroner's court in charge of investigating the causes of death. In short, the law was summoned to establish the discriminatory nature of the local police approach. During the audience at the coroner's court and in presence of the five silent youths who could not be judged again having been previously found innocent, for the first time the jury members qualified these youths' action as murder during a racist, entirely unprovoked action. By mere luck, a journalist from the *Daily Mail* covered the audience, and soon turned public opinion in favor of the victim's family.

The way the police conducted the investigation led the family, supported by the Commission on racial equality and by 19 Parliament members, to file a complaint. In the meantime, the Labour Party had won the elections and in 1997, Jack Straw, at the head of the Home Office, required retired judge Sir William MacPherson to establish the facts. The latter convened militants and specialists of racial relations and listened to them. After 60 days of audits, in February 1999, an 11,000-page report circulated on the Internet, pointed at "a combination of professional incompetence, institutional racism and a failure of leadership by senior officers" (MacPherson, 1999: 46.1). It asserted that the crime was racially motivated. The inability of officers of all ranks to understand how "race" might be embedded in police work was obvious. While racism in the police force was not overt, institutional racism was defined as "the collective failure of an organization to provide an appropriated and professional service to people because of their colour, culture, or ethnic origin. It can be seen or detected in processes, attitudes and behaviour, which amount to discrimination, through unwitting prejudice, ignorance, thoughtlessness, and racist stereotyping which disadvantage minority ethnic people. It persists because of the failure of the organization openly and adequately to recognize and address its existence and causes by policy, example and leadership. Without recognition and action to eliminate such racism, it can prevail as part of the ethos or culture of the organization. It is a corrosive disease" (MacPherson, 1999: 6.34).

The 70 recommendations in the report, with 39 of them specifically addressed to the police, were influential. The report advocated new procedures on reporting and investigating racist crimes; it tightened the rules for stop-and-search practices, emphasized the importance of culturally diversifying the police force, and made racist behavior in the police an offense leading to the dismissal of the offender. "A racist officer is an incompetent officer," the report stressed (1999: 332). It urged for the creation of an independent police complaints system. The Home Office took the report seriously. A Lawrence Steering Group was created including minority representatives, the police, and other agencies.

The MacPherson report was a fundamental vehicle of the police response to diversity issues. The *Race Relations (Amendment) Act* 2000 required all public authorities, including the police, to be proactive in addressing issues of discrimination and fair treatment. It concerned "hard to reach" communities as well, living on the fringes of society who had differing needs and were ignored by the mainstream. The Commission on Racial Equality was accountable for the implementation of dozens of antidiscriminatory measures involving the police force.

But within the police, the report triggered confusion and anger. Many police officers refused to be labeled racist and distanced themselves from the local police patrol which had been charged with misconduct in the Lawrence case. As his French and American counterparts would have, a British police officer testifying during the audience explained that in practice, police officers' encounters with minority youths are less motivated by racism than by frustrating experiences, "if the predominantly white staff of the police organization have their experience of visible minorities largely restricted to interactions with such groups, then negative racial stereotypes will tend to develop accordingly" (MacPherson, 1999: 6–31).

The report's recommendations also raised a number of problems, in particular in matters of stop and search already correlated with racial profiling for a lot of young minority males. What were the police to do? Could the police be efficient without the consent of those controlled? If not, were identity checks to be suspended? A majority of the Londoners thought that they were efficient and could lead to drug or weapons seizure.

The 1839 law on the Metropolitan police allowed the British police to control individuals with a "reasonable suspicion" to do so. Recently, such controls have taken place in a preventative approach in problem neighborhoods. Lord Scarman had pointed at them for creating tensions in Brixton. After a wide police search called Swamp 81 meant to put an end to muggings, they led to the arrests of a majority of blacks who only made 12% of the population and three quarters of youths under 21 years old. For Reiner (1985), a specialist of the British police, most surveys revealed that police harassment always came first, before structural causes such as unemployment, poor housing, poverty, and marginalization on reasons for rioting among participants.

The 1984 law—*Police and Criminal Evidence Act* (Pace)—allowed all police forces to detain an individual briefly, short of arrest, make inquiries, and undertake a personal search in order to confirm or allay a reasonable suspicion that the person has committed or is about to commit a criminal offence. But for those who are searched, this definition remains vague and illegitimate. This approach is perceived as "a means of 'social control,' intelligence collection, breaking up groups of young people and a general deterrent for which there is no basis in law." It offends "the rights to freedom of movement, privacy and respect for personal liberty" (Bowling, 2007: 25). Its efficiency is questionable. Of every 100 recorded searches "on suspicion," about 88 are fruitless; that is, they do not result in an arrest for the behavior suspected or for any other reason (Home Office, 2005). The basis for "reasonable suspicion often turns out to be absent … and police officers fail to distinguish those involved in a crime from urban males wearing hooded sweat-shirts, for example" (Bowling, 2007: 26). These findings are also found in France and in the US. A majority of offences are solved as a result of information coming from the public. For the Home Office, stop-and-search has only a limited disruptive impact on crime by intercepting those going to commit an offense … and it is unlikely that searches make a substantial contribution to undermining drug markets or drug-related crime (Miller et al., 2000). After 1993, authorities decided that police tickets had to mention the reason for control and the race and ethnicity of the person stopped. A copy had to be given to the latter.

The dilemma for the police comes, on the one hand, from the over-representation of minorities among suspects: they are stopped six to seven times more frequently by the police than others but the result in arrests is typically around 12% and it can fall as low as 7%, showing that the suspicion is unfounded nine times out of ten (Bowling, 2007: 28). Yet on the other hand, the police have to respond to the major concern of Londoners about crime linked to drugs and young men carrying knives. "Stopping people in a public place and searching them *in situ* is a particular hot topic in many jurisdictions because it is believed that visible minorities are treated selectively. In Britain, it has been referred to 'disproportionality,' elsewhere in the Anglo-Saxon world it is more commonly known as 'racial profiling' or colloquially, as 'walking/driving while black' … indicates how suspicion alights more easily upon

DOI: 10.1057/9781137428004.0006

some sections of the population than others...it may be equally due to differences between segments of the population in their use of public space. However what is undoubtedly true in most, if not all, jurisdictions is that those stopped and searched are disproportionately young men" (Waddington, 2009: 282). As rightfully remarked by Waddington (2009), driving is not a right, but an activity *permitted* or *licensed* by the state under certain conditions. Police are in their right if they stop and search a vehicle, take samples of the driver's breath, and decide to let him/her go. They may cordon off areas of public space and restrict access to those who consent to be searched. Controversy comes from the unreasonable or lack of suspicion in the stop and search of the police, from the profiling, and from the manner in which the search is conducted.

Other courts' decisions

Disproportionality has become more apparent in the contexts of post-9/11 and post-7/7 terrorist attacks, after which anti-immigrant hostility increased. Radical organizations perceived as risk were banned, troublesome places of worship closed, and pretrial hearings held in "secret" courts.

British courts and various dissenting bodies attempted to alleviate the governments' aim at restricting the civil liberties of risk groups for the sake of order. The example that comes to mind is that of citizens of immigrant origin certified as terrorists by the Home Secretary but who could not be deported. They could have been detained in prison without trial forever. But in 2005, the House of Lords argued that this measure was discriminatory because it could not apply to British citizens. The Lords said that Britain's response was disproportionate since it affected only non-nationals. The High Court also vetoed six Control orders from the government disrespectful of the European Convention on Human Rights. This resistance did not prevent policies of repression from developing (as seen with the restrictive measures taken against immigration, a general trend in Europe).

The Menendez case, a Brazilian electrician, killed wrongly on a subway platform by the London Metropolitan police after the London attacks of July 7, 2005, eventually cost its commissioner Ian Blair, his position, showing that British justice keeps its leverage and requires accountability from political elites. Currently, stop and search remains controversial in Britain. At the beginning of 2014, as in the US (but not in France), there was a Court Challenge about the legality of police activity in this area.

DOI: 10.1057/9781137428004.0006

In the end, the Court came down on the side of police and that decision rose stimulated controversy.

The British police have also been shaken by a public inquiry reporting, in 2014, that members of the Special Demonstration Squad, a secret police unit established to infiltrate protest groups, employed an undercover officer to spy on the Stephen Lawrence family with the goal of discrediting it, if it pressed for justice. "Despite (its) history of corruption, prejudice and injustice, the police have never faced such a crisis of confidence and trust as today," remarks lecturer K. Malik. "Today, as the old conflicts have ebbed away, the role of Britain's police is far less clear," it no longer safeguards the stability of British society and its institutions and police officers find themselves facing a crisis of identity and authority (Malik, 2014).

The strength of antidiscrimination struggles in Britain

It is probably in Britain that the link between public (dis)order and minorities' social integration in a multicultural society is the strongest. As seen in the previous chapter, the country has experienced public disorders involving young people and the police every decade. These events have been followed by Parliamentary debates, official reports, laws, and governmental measures. Reports "conceptualize the links between racial diversity and urban violence and they contribute to an evaluation of integration and citizenship in a multicultural society" (Garbaye, 2011: 11, 15). The Scarman report established a correlation between disorders, minorities, and police brutality, reinforcing the weight of the race relations perspective and of multiculturalism. It advocated antidiscrimination struggles. Targeting racial minorities, it urged for "positive actions" in their favor, already recommended by the *Race Relations Act of 1976*. It meant that local authorities could fix objectives for the recruitment of minorities, in particular in the police and for the allocation of funds, according to the size of the minority populations in the localities. It pleaded in favor of racial statistics and denounced the underrepresentation of minorities in institutions. It encouraged investigations to detect indirect forms of discrimination, with the help of ethnic monitoring (Garbaye, 2009: 44).

The trend to the racialization of disorders was boosted by both political rhetoric and by the media, in the 1980s. The MacPherson report, establishing the notion of institutional racism, established that racism was not just caused by persons but by institutions as well. It was followed

DOI: 10.1057/9781137428004.0006

by the third *Race Relations Act* in 2000, amplifying antidiscrimination options. But then, after the 2001 disorders, official reports (Cantle, Denham) suggested that multiculturalism allowed, or even created the development of communities segregated by race and ethnicity in British society. The Cantle report (2001) points at "parallel lives" preventing any form of understanding between whites and Asians.

Regarding racism, Amin (2003) remarks that the British context has significantly changed and that this change had an impact on the 2001 disorders. When the Labour Party returned to power in 1997, after the Lawrence case, there was a strong denunciation of discriminations and of hate crimes which stirred the public debate. That such an issue was publicly discussed, Amin says, reveals a form of minority integration in British culture. It implies that belonging and citizenship cannot be reduced to the markers of white race and to Old English values. He stresses that, in parallel, nevertheless, the Thatcherite legacy persists, emphasizing "the strangeness of Otherness." It is within that trend that national reactions to the 2001 disorders belong; they question cultural practices and the national belonging of British Muslims, a question met by the support to the National Front (Body-Gendrot, 2012: 154). Amin's remarks proved true and the disorders of 2011 were not identified as "race riots." Community cohesion was advocated.

The two logics, multiculturalism and community cohesion, are contradictory (Garbaye, 2009: 87). Communities need to strengthen their resources before they can bond with other communities. But in the meanwhile, separatism persists, leadership and networking are inward-oriented, and the patrolling of community boundaries, in particular, persists. Community cohesion may also appear as an injunction to cultural assimilation. It is likely that the European Union urging policies of equal opportunity influenced such orientation, diverting it from an exclusive focus on race relations and more on common values.

American experiences

Former research on police identity checks

The racial riots of the 1960s pushed President L.B. Johnson to summon a commission of investigation under the chairmanship of Judge Otto Kerner. It produced a seminal report from the National Advisory Commission on Civil Disorders (1968). The report's basic conclusion was that "Our Nation is moving towards two societies, one black, one white-separate and unequal." It pointed at the failures of institutions, government, schools, social policies and to forms of abuse, brutality, and institutional racism from the police toward racial minorities which could lead the latter to collective violence. The overrepresentation of Afro-Americans among victims of police shootings was proved. Between 1976 and 1987, 1,800 blacks died under such circumstances (three times more than whites). As observed by the author of *Race, Space and Riots*, Janet Abu-Lughod, "Particularly in the 1990s, the issue of police brutality had come up time and again in cities all over the country. There is no question that 'targeting' of minorities, whether based on scientifically derived profiles of probability or upon racist assumptions of policemen (who in most cities with large minority proportions, are still predominantly white) is a fact of the contemporary period" (2007: 32). By comparison, between 2000 and 2005, five individuals a year were killed by the French police. Among those, Arabs or their descent were overrepresented (Jobard, 2003). Following the publishing of the Kerner report, subsequent pressures were exerted on the police in order to alleviate ethnoracial profiling and police abuse and the hiring of more minority policemen was undertaken. However, by 1999 and after serious antipolice demonstrations following the notorious Diallo case, an innocent black student labelled peddler by the media and being killed by a patrol of the street crime unit, such unit was dismantled. Yet, despite promises for reforms, the police force was still 67% white, whereas all minorities made more than 65% of the city's population. Only after 9/11 and the deaths of numerous policemen creating an unusual number of vacancies, were minority recruits boosted (Abu-Lughod, 2007: 31).

Police identity checks in New York

In 1999, after minority representatives took New York City to court for discriminatory practices (*Daniels et al. v. The City of New York*), the prosecutor of the state, Eliot Spitzer, became aware that African-Americans made half of those stopped and searched. In many African-American communities, the racial breach had prevented police–citizen cooperation. Minorities' distrust of the police was partly reduced in 2003, after the New York Police Department (NYPD) signed a consent decree prohibiting the practice of racial profiling. An investigation relative to the street crime unit, led by US attorney-general M.J. White, confirmed the results found by New York State attorney-general Eliot Spitzer: African-

DOI: 10.1057/9781137428004.0006

Americans, 25% of the population, made up half of those stopped, Latinos, 25% of the population, were one-third of those stopped, while whites, 43.4% of the population, were 13% of those stopped. The City of New York then agreed to spend $1.5 million in the creation of files to evaluate the fairness of NYPD procedures. It became mandatory for state and city police forces to indicate the ethnic or racial origin of the searched person on the ticket following a stop. All the tickets were sent to the central computerized system and processed electronically in order to check whether there was an overrepresentation of racial minorities and if that was so, who was responsible. Often, the street crime unit, moved by a performance culture, would be.

Nevertheless, as in England, the trauma caused by 9/11 and the need to trust the police for more protection alleviated the constraints put on the NYPD. The concept of *reasonable suspicion* (never precisely defined) led courts to grant more leverage to the police.[1] Deciding whether the alleged criminals' human dignity had been preserved or not during police stops and searches, courts looked more at what harm was done than at what should have been the required procedure according to the law (Harcourt, 2001). In what he calls "the indignities of order maintenance policing," Fagan (2011), a professor at Columbia Law School and an expert on police discrimination, points out that a new body of research indicates that, in numerous American cities, police interactions with citizens, especially with frequently stopped minority citizens, are hostile and aggressive. His argument is that a widespread use of coercive police authority harms citizens' dignity. The American Constitution combines both notions of respect and dignity. The Fourth Amendment protects the fundamentals of human dignity for defendants. For Fagan, such police searches without reasonable cause bring up emotions such as humiliation and rage which are detrimental to trust in the police force. "Public shaming" and verbal degradation are particularly resented by black young men who are the most frequently stopped. In New York, minorities, then, organized themselves so that their complaints would be heard by the greatest numbers. Reverend Al Sharpton became a famous leader in antipolice demonstrations and used this success to run for mayor later on.

The enforcement of Fourth Amendment rights has changed over time in favor of crime control. The police found suspects, even when the signals of a crime afoot were weak. In 2005, police stopped more than one in ten adult citizens over the age of 16, including stops on highways and pedestrian stops (Fagan and Meares, 2008). Moreover, until 2010 when a suit was filed, stop records were stored in huge database by the NYPD, even when there was no evidence that a crime had been committed and any law enforcer had access to them.

Almost 600,000 New Yorkers were stopped in 2009 (three times the number in 2003); 473,000 of them were what the New York Civil Liberties Union (NYCLU) calls "innocent New Yorkers."

Unsurprisingly, the five police precincts where most minorities live were those with the greatest number of police stops. Four out of five stops were located in Brooklyn. From 2003 to 2009, blacks and Hispanics combined were stopped nine times more than whites and made 85% of all stops (Center for Constitutional Rights memorandum, February 24, 2010).

The most frequent reason given by police officers for initiating a stop is not the suspicion that individuals are carrying a gun or their physical appearance but in almost half of the cases, that they were engaged in "furtive movements." This is a highly ambiguous and ill-defined notion, also used by the French police. But less than 2% of all the stops resulted in the discovery of a weapon (gun, knife, and so on) and in the possession of some kind of contraband, including illegal drugs. Just 6% of the stops ended with an arrest in 2008 (Center for Constitutional Rights memorandum, February 24, 2010: 10). The rationale given by Police Commissioner W. Bratton in 1994 with regard to the number-one strategy, "Getting Guns off the streets of New York" and "Reclaiming the public spaces" did not seem justified in light of the following numbers: 627 guns were recovered in 2003 and 824 in 2008. In raw numbers, over 300,000 stops of blacks yielded only 617 guns; 135,000 stops of Hispanics, 121 guns and 57,000 stops of whites, 42 guns (*ibid.*, 18). Force was about 20% more likely to be used against black than white suspects, once the characteristics of the stop were controlled.

The courts' decisions

Whether institutions can act efficiently when most citizens think society is unfair remains a basic question. The minimal constitutional requirements that the Supreme Court put in place follow the 1968 *Terry v. Ohio* decision. For a stop, there must be reasonable and articulable suspicion that a person is engaged in a crime and for a frisk, reasonable and articulable suspicion that a person is armed and dangerous. In 2008, the Centre for Constitutional Rights filed a new complaint in federal court accusing

DOI: 10.1057/9781137428004.0006

the NYPD once more of failing to include essential details on required police forms to show whether the stops were justified. Minorities disproportionately endured more adversarial contacts with the police than similarly situated whites. In more that 30% of the stops, the proof of reasonable suspicion necessary to make the stop constitutional was lacking. The challenge to the legitimacy of police action led to a class action lawsuit, *Floyd v. The City of New York* (2011) during which minority men and women testified for several months. In July 2013, in a 195-page decision, a federal judge, Judge Shira A. Scheindlin, found that the Police Department resorted to a "policy of indirect racial profiling," leading officers to routinely stop blacks and Hispanics who would not have been stopped if they were white. She ruled that the policing strategy violated the constitutional rights of minority New Yorkers and demonstrated a widespread disregard for the Fourteenth Amendment which protects against unreasonable searches and seizures by the government as well for the Fourth Amendment's equal protection clause.

Mayor Michael R. Bloomberg and police commissioner Raymond Kelly defended stop-and-frisk tactics as an invaluable crime-fighting tool, one that city officials insist has helped cut crime in New York to record lows. Guns and drugs were major problems in the inner city and stops appear as a legitimate way to address them, they said. Claiming that the city had not been given a fair trial, the mayor appealed the decision both in the court of appeals and the court of public opinion and Judge Scheindlin was forced to withdraw from the case. But her recommendations were maintained.

First, a pilot program would be launched, and officers in at least five precincts across the city would wear cameras on their bodies to record street encounters. The judge also ordered a "joint remedial process," that is, a series of community meetings to solicit public comments on how to reform the Police Department's tactics. Then a former prosecutor was asked to supervise reform and monitor the Police Department's compliance with the US Constitution.

Whether this landmark decision restored trust in the police in the inner city and allowed better cooperation is beyond the scope of this research. The new mayor, elected in Fall 2013, Bill de Blasio, has campaigned on reforming stop-and-frisk practices and his new police chief, William Bratton (formerly the police chief of Mayor Giuliani, then the police chief of Los Angeles), has condemned them as causing alienation in the minority community. Instead, he has advocated "collaborative" policing. Knowing

DOI: 10.1057/9781137428004.0006

who is in the community, good and bad people, and how to interact with them was the challenge faced by Sir Robert Peel over 150 years ago as it is today, the police chief mentioned in a public speech in January 2014.

One may remain doubtful, however. Young black men (and some not so young), who have borne the brunt of the stops, said they had little hope that even as the rule book of stop-and-frisk policing changed, the practice would change along with it. Distrust of the police keeps running deep in poor black neighborhoods for some reason. In some neighborhoods, almost all adults have been to jail. Reverend Al Sharpton, the African-American community activist, remarked in a press conference in 2014 that W. Peel in the 1820s was not dealing with the diversity that one finds in 21st century New York and that "we are not born in this kind of world" (Apuzzo and Goldstein, 2014). It is well known among the police that stops and searches do not impact crime: when the number of stops dropped by 20% in 2012, for example, there was no corresponding rise in homicides in New York. Only the "focused deterrence" strategy targeting the few individuals who are typically responsible for driving up crime produces noteworthy differences.

Racial minorities' inequality of treatment by justice

For the author of *No Equal Justice*, the poor and black in America receive unequal justice, not only are they more frequently stopped and searched and arrested six times the rate of white men, they have lower quality attorneys for their defense, unfair juries, greater rates of conviction, and longer sentences for similar crimes and as said before, they are more often the victims of the police use of deadly force (Cole, 2012). For Cole, "while our criminal justice system is explicitly based on the premise and promise of equality before the law, the administration of criminal law…is in fact predicated on the exploitation of inequality…(O)ur criminal justice system affirmatively depends on inequality. Absent race and class disparities, the privileged among us could not enjoy as much constitutional protection of our liberties as we do; and without those disparities, we could not afford the policy of mass incarceration that we have pursued over the past two decades."

"Get tough" politics on crime and drugs have animated American social policy for three generations. The national level has taken over what used to be local issues of law and order and launched major campaigns on drugs, withholding funds from states unless they accepted repressive measures favored by conservative majorities in Congress. For example,

DOI: 10.1057/9781137428004.0006

"truth in sentencing" under which inmates are required to serve at least 85% of their time addressed only 8% of inmates, those in federal prisons. Congress exerted pressures on states where inmates generally served 48% of their sentences and gave them incentives via increased funding to impose 85% of the sentences. This move in response to populist demands can be seen as a significant federalization of a traditional local issue (Body-Gendrot, 2000: 48). Instead of weighing mitigating circumstances as used to be the case before sentencing, henceforth judges had also their hands tied up by mandatory sentencing.

As a counterpart for their acquiescence, counties and cities received billions of dollars. From 1965 to 1992, federal expenditures for justice programs almost quadrupled. When President Nixon made his fight on crime a national priority in 1970, his budget tripled to $900 billion. Local spending on police protection leapt from $2,001 billion in 1965 to $6,813 billion in 1975 and by 1995 it had reached $58,768 billion. As for the cost of incarceration, state governments took most of the expenditures. Their costs increased from $632 billion in 1965 to $2,193 billion in 1975 and reached $4,258 billion in 1980 (Katz, 2012: 92). President Clinton, a Democrat, followed the same trend offering the states $1.5 billion if they followed the new standards of harshness in the way they treated any juvenile charged with a violent crime and judged as an adult, unless a state attorney-general decided otherwise.

What such figures reveal is that the goal of such measures was less concrete results in public action than being on the contested terrain of law and order, with battles fought over power and principle among politicians, at all kinds of levels. Some of them were moved by ideology and others by mere electoral calculation. As a result, 3,000 crimes were transformed into federal offenses revealing how much Congress wanted to get hold of the crime issue.

Urban African-Americans were the targets of such repressive orientations. They "have borne the brunt of the War on Drugs. They have been arrested, prosecuted, convicted, and imprisoned at increasing rates since the early 1980s and grossly out of proportion to their numbers in the general population or among drug users" (Tonry, 1995: 105). At the height of the war on drugs in 1989, five times more blacks were arrested than whites despite the fact that their drug consumption was the same, but not in the same manner. Blacks would use crack cocaine visibly on the streets, making their arrests by the police easier, while whites would consume cocaine at home or in their office.

DOI: 10.1057/9781137428004.0006

Why was this harsh and costly policy preferred to that of prevention as advocated by President L.B. Johnson? The politicization of the law and order issue, the management of polarization, and the conservatism of elected elites are part of the explanation. Racism is another. Under the Reagan Administration, the "underclass" was an artifact constructed for political purposes. Black males were portrayed as a dangerous, dysfunctional, young, impulsive, hostile category in the media and these disturbing images contributed to externalize them as if they were not part of society. For Wilson (1987) who stopped using the term, two major changes led to create this "underclass": first the deindustrialization of American cities placing stable jobs out of reach for inner-city residents (lots of them with no cars); second, the bifurcation of minority communities, the most mobile leaving the inner cities and leaving isolated the poorest. This latter category has no allies, it inspires fear (Body-Gendrot, 2000: 34). Without resources, a lot of them become homeless or double up with family or friends. Their survival strategies make them frequently move from one residence to another in order to find temporary support systems. Cutbacks in social services from conservative legislatures are a major cause of increased homelessness. Numerous ex-convicts (one black out of four) are without resources and forced into paths of repeated crime. As a consequence, inner cities with poor minority residents remain under heavy police and penitentiaries' surveillance.

Muslims as a "suspect category"[2]

In the ten years following 9/11, numerous Northern European countries responded with a more punitive rhetoric, the development of the precautionary principle, and tougher criminal decisions. Yet Europeans are not Americans. Differences of scale and nature and intensity in choices of measures are noteworthy. One should distinguish at which levels politicians waving the red flag operate, and according to which culture and structures they are able to do so. "Suppose we don't act and the intelligence turns out to be right, how forgiving will people be?" T. Blair exclaimed (quoted in Crawford, 2011: 14). National culture makes a difference. The reason why Muslims are introduced in this issue of policing the inner city does not come from their geographical location in the poorer areas of cities, although in the cases of France and Britain, they may. Their lack of integration is seen as a problem, more in Britain than elsewhere. A German Marshall Fund poll from 2011 shows that if for 45% of the French and of Americans, Muslims are integrating well, only 37% of the British

DOI: 10.1057/9781137428004.0006

think so (Schain, 2012: 19). The justification of including Muslims in this research also comes from the fact that they become "clients" of police forces under specific circumstances such as threats of terrorism, a factor which may make them belong to "visible minorities."

Paris

Paris is a well-policed city. Whenever it is anticipated that disorders could occur (during street demonstrations or massive celebrations, for instance), a strong paramilitary police deployment is efficiently in charge of law and order; 1,100 policemen currently patrol trains and thousands of cameras have been added for surveillance and identification in the Parisian region. The Vigipirate program in France, created in 1974, was reinforced after terrorist attacks hit the country in the 1990s. Armed soldiers exert surveillance on railway stations, airports, and other sensitive public places. Databases contain files on an increasing number of people and when errors are made or when someone has been cleared by police or justice, it is very difficult for anyone to extract his/her name from the database. Moreover, the driving force behind such public policy of control is traceability. A symbol is sent to the public that state authorities are watching citizens' behavior and protecting them as well.

While terrorism threatening the city is not a topic discussed by the media, youth violence in the *banlieues* projects is. It is a useful metaphor to address a cocktail of fears, malaises, and tensions in French society. Should a terrorist attack shake Paris and France, they would then be forgotten in the political and media discourses, or on the contrary, they would appear as a sort of Fifth column threatening national security.

Terrorist attacks as early as 1954–1962, during the "Algerian war," with the case of the Secret Army Organization penetrating security forces, generated a specific legislation. But when terrorist attacks hit France again in the mid-1980s, the governing elites showed reluctance to enact special legislation. Domestic terrorism was fought by the agency for international surveillance, by the Head of the territorial security (DST), and by the counterespionage service SDECE. In 1986, 14 terrorist acts were committed in the names of the Committee of Solidarity with Arabic and Middle East Political Prisoners. The first antiterrorism statute was passed in 1986. It had taken about 15 years to the counterterrorism unit (UCLAT) to function properly. Legislators chose to adapt ordinary criminal law and procedures based on the enforcement of specific rules to fight terrorism. (It was the position defended after 9/11.)

DOI: 10.1057/9781137428004.0006

But when in 1995 and in 1996, the Algerian radical Islamism Organization (GIA) launched new terrorist attacks, a new antiterrorism statute adjusted to the evolution of terrorism and provided enforcement agencies with the required tools. Although terrorism became an obsession for French authorities in charge of territorial security, however, a national silence about terrorism threats and new risks characterized the French approach (with the exception of Minister of Interior Sarkozy warning the French in 2005 that the risk of violent action on the land was real and the threat serious). Europol stated in 2008 that France was probably, after Spain, the member state of the EU most concerned by a terrorist threat. Such a context explains in part why, in national polls, the French express a suspicion regarding Arabs and Muslims in general, by comparison with previous waves of immigration.

As the capital of the country, the City of Paris' preventative and territorialized strategies are blurred with those of the state. They could be summarized, as depending from a highly centralized command at the top of a security pyramid relying more heavily on human resources in the field than on technologies.

This territorial strategy goes along with a second strategy, focused on individuals. The French intelligence services have a fairly good knowledge and experience of the Arabic–Muslim world due, in great part, to a long cooperation with the intelligence services in North African countries. With the largest Muslim population in Europe, some members of whom are radicalized, France experiences a continuous risk of home-grown or external terrorism (Mehra and Menouch cases). For years, as in the two other countries studied here, French intelligence services have infiltrated and exerted surveillance on radical extremist groups in 300 risk neighborhoods around Paris (Body-Gendrot and Spierenburg, 2008).

Several criteria determine what a sensitive zone is for the intelligence service, among them an important number of immigrants; ethnic stores; non-Western and religious ways of dressing; radical imams, etc. This surveillance is justified by the services, as it is estimated in 2014 that at least 900 French have joined the Jihad and fight Western army forces in beleaguered countries. It is worth mentioning that, where the US and Britain have recently dismantled their units spying on Muslims under pressure from progressive organizations, such is not the case in France.

From field observations, information trickles up to the Police Prefect, the territorial security direction (DST), the judiciary police, and various

DOI: 10.1057/9781137428004.0006

branches allowing antiterrorist judges to indict the right people. When suspicion is beyond a "reasonable doubt," after intelligence services' investigation, under the claim of health and safety checks or of a tax audit, undercover round-ups take place. The number of deportations fluctuates according to politics. It was low in 2013 with a Left government in power. The state agencies, less than the Police Prefect, have the upper hand as safety is a sovereign domain of the central state. However, stripping those found guilty of their citizenship, as English government would like to do, does not seem an option in France, despite growing support given to the National Front's ideas. Although the media exacerbate fears of Islamist extremists, it is unlikely that politicians will take the risk of antagonizing French Muslims who are the largest community in Europe. In 2010, J. Barrot, the chair of the section Justice, Liberty and Security at the European Community, took steps to avoid the stigmatization of Muslims in general. Following the positions taken by the French state, his position was that Islam should be seen less as a source of conflict than as a means of integration in Europe. This cautious attitude was not observed for the Romas, however. Their stigmatization by the French government in 2010 created an embarrassment for France within the European Commission.

London

On July 7, 2005, three near-simultaneous suicide attacks were launched by British Muslims from Leeds on the London Underground and one hour later, on a double-decker bus. The offenders were carrying backpacks loaded with 5–12 lb of explosives; 56 people were killed, including the terrorists themselves, and 450 persons were wounded. The cameras allowed the identification of home-grown Muslim terrorists who lived in Leeds and led "quiet" lives there, making the understanding of their motivations at that time difficult.

At the request of former British Prime Minister Gordon Brown, citizens, local communities, institutions, and firms were required to tackle, to uproot the evils that threaten to drive people, particularly vulnerable young people into the hands of violent extremists.

The fear of new terrorist attacks legitimated territorial surveillance as a first strategy. As in New York, the use of new technologies of surveillance, control and identification, and a policy meant to secure public spaces in London were developed via new schemes. A lot of the CCTVs were already deployed in London. The decision of deploying more cameras was more symbolic than efficient, although they were very useful again in August 2011 (Body-Gendrot 2012, ch.3).

Rapidly, the London landscape, as that of New York and Paris, changed after 9/11. "Walls and defences are social order, written into material form, a key feature for the understanding of human territoriality," Coaffee et al. remark (2009: 21).[3] Exclusion zones are provided to protect at-risk sites and managerial measures to regulate the public crowd. Discipline is imposed by required passwords and electronic cards to enter certain spaces and social worlds. CCTVs were first introduced in 1985 in a resort town, Bournemouth, after a bomb had been thrown during a Conservative Party Conference in Brighton, almost killing Prime Minister Thatcher. Casinos had installed them in the US to prevent fraud in the 1960s. Then they moved to malls and theme parks. Fighting hooliganism, the UK became a pioneer for urban spatial control in Europe. CCTVs are currently estimated at 4.2 million, one for every 14 people. Every day, someone in Britain may be identified 300 times (Coaffee et al., 2009: 80)? CCTVs proliferate in public spaces, and the security issue continuously adds more requirements. The famous remark made by Information Commissioner R. Thomas in 2004: "we are sleepwalking into a surveillance society" comes to mind. Technological options prevail over those of social inclusion. There is a lack of awareness from citizens that, resorting to technology, threatens the very essence of what a city is, that is "making society."

The second strategy is to exert surveillance on Muslims.

The "suspect community" issue[4]

It is difficult to conduct a comparative survey on Muslims. A Gallup 2006–2007 survey and other sources show why these comparisons are difficult. First of all, only British census collects voluntary religious affiliation. Second of all, Muslims' numbers and origins vary: in France they are estimated to be four million, in Germany three million and in the UK, 1.6 million. In London they comprise 8.5% of the population, 607,000 are South Asians, 24% Bangladeshis, 22% Pakistanis, 7% Indians. In Paris they make 7.8%, 1.6 million are North Africans, 239,000 Africans, 50,000 Turks. Inside communities, diversity prevails (new Muslim groups in London come from East Africa, Guiana and Trinidad, their incomes vary (Bangladeshi are low income compared with Indians who are more affluent).

According to a Pew Research investigation in 2006, religion is central to the identity of European Muslims. With the exception of Muslims

DOI: 10.1057/9781137428004.0006

in France who consider themselves equally as Muslims/French and are the most integrative in their orientations, Muslims identify primarily as Muslims (81%) rather than as British (7%), Spanish (89/3), or German (66/13) (42% of American Christians identify first as Christians and not Americans); 72% of French Muslims have no conflict between being devout and living in a modern country but 49% of British Muslims do; 60% of the former are secular integrationists versus 10.7% of the latter (Schain, 2012: 20).

According to Tyler, the relationship that British Muslims have with authorities such as the police is not based on deterrence but on "consent" acquired from their perception and experience of fairness. Their cooperation is rooted in social relations and in ethical judgment, and not in legitimacy per se. A Gallup World poll in 2007 (Table 4.1) reveals their confidence in institutions, and the lack of interference from religious practices. Considering such data, the suspicion in which Muslims are held in public opinions appears unjustified. Greer (2010) suggests banning the expression "suspect community" as applied to Muslims in the UK, once again illustrating sharp differences from a legal standpoint between Britain, the US, and France.

Greer takes issue with an article by Pantazis and Pemberton defining a suspect community as "a sub-group of the population that is singled out for state attention as being 'problematic.' Specifically, in terms of policing, individuals may be targeted, not necessarily as a result of suspected wrong doing, but simply because of their presumed membership to (sic) that sub-group. Race, ethnicity, religion, class, gender, language, accent, dress, political ideology or any combination of these factors may serve to delineate the sub-group" (2009: 649). For these authors, the *Terrorism Act 2000* in Britain has "largely facilitated the designation of Muslims as the principal suspect community" (*ibid.*: 652) allowing the police to

TABLE 4.1   *Muslims in Paris and London having confidence in democratic institutions (%)*

	Justice	National government	Media
Muslims in Paris	49	40	35
French population	48	36	34
Muslims in London	67	64	51
British population	55	36	41

Source: Zsolt Nyiri, Gallup World Poll (2007).

DOI: 10.1057/9781137428004.0006

stop and search at random (sections 44 and 45). "A 'community' can be considered to be under official suspicion if, and only if, a substantial majority of those who share its identity are under official suspicion, and/ or if this identity is, in and of itself, sufficient to arouse systematic official suspicion" (Greer, 2010: 1178). The number of those stopped in 2001–2002 rose from 10,200 individuals to 256,026 in 2008–2009, after the attacks. According to the 2009 Home Office Statistical Bulletin, 2% of the stops were carried out by the Metropolitan police service. Greer established a distinction between "feeling under suspicion," "being under official suspicion," and "being under unjustified suspicion." If young middle class men from Leeds with Pakistani background carrying backpacks in a railway station were suspected by the police of being troublemakers, such "official" suspicion is justified for Greer. He contests, however, the reference to Muslims who, themselves, are divided by race, ethnicity, national origins, and demographic factors. Out of 2 million, 70% live in London, Birmingham, Manchester, and Bradford-Leeds (Peach, 2006: 631, 650). Salafism and Islamism are ideologies, not communities, Greer remarks. When the British police stop blacks and Asians, their religion is not recorded and no one knows (as in France) how many among them are Muslim. If there is suspicion in some areas that plots are designed, they are closely monitored by the Office of Security and Counter-terrorism, more so because they contain critical infrastructures or places of national significance than because they are in Muslim neighborhoods. In Greater London which is at risk of terrorism, police powers are legally restrained. Community impact assessment is a vital part of the police authorization process and officers required to keep careful records. With such tight monitoring, and despite racial unbalance in the stops and searches, there is no evidence that racial profiling is an effective counter-terrorist strategy (Greer, *ibid.*: 1182).

The European Convention of Human Rights (ECHR) (and also France) does not support the suspect community thesis either, yet it admits that blacks and Asians are four times more likely than their white counterparts to be stopped and searched.

In the case *Gillan v. Commissioner of Police for the Metropolis and Secretary of State for the Home*, the House of Lords unanimously held that stops and searches are not based on racial profiling alone. The Prevent Program allowing a lot of leverage to policemen from the Home Office was terminated in July 2010. It was indeed criticized for its mixture of *trust* and *suspicion*, in particular when over 150 automatic number plate

DOI: 10.1057/9781137428004.0006

recognition cameras were about to be installed in two predominantly Muslim neighborhoods of Birmingham as part of counterterrorism strategies. That the neighborhoods were Muslim had less to do with race and ethnicity than with a specific plot aimed at killing a British soldier in the area, Greer explains. The Prevent Program was investigated by the House of Commons Select Committee on Communities and Local Government. The report published in March 2010 questions methods of "spying," "surveillance," and "intelligence gathering," hiding a variety of doubtful interpretations. The Head of the Home Office himself, D. Blunkett, asked British people not to yield to fear and not to exaggerate the terrorist threat. This attitude was very different from that of the US attorney-general, mobilizing citizens as "spies" to denounce suspects and suspicious activities in their community to authorities (most citizens did not) and poles apart from the French position making politically incorrect the term "délation" (denunciation) since World War II.

Pantazis and Pemberton claim that high-profile police raids, arrests, and detention of Muslim terrorist suspects generate fear, creating strong feelings of dislike among non-Muslims (2009: 661). But for Greer, while Muslim communities as a whole are not systematically represented as suspect, extremist sections within them are. The *Racial and Religious Hatred Act* of 2006 seeks to protect Muslims from hate crimes. Most Muslims and their leaders support official policies fighting terrorism. Research shows, indeed, that crime is concentrated at very small geographic units of analysis. A focus on procedures can help the police identify behavior, tactics, and strategies that many members of minority communities find problematic, leading to disaffection, even though the behaviors, tactics, and strategies may seem lawful and, considered in isolation, effective. It is important not to neglect the psychological aspects of legitimacy in individual encounters, and the issue of respect, whether it is shown or not, by the police is recurrent in interviews with minorities.

In 2014, the power to strip dual citizens of their British rights—habeas corpus and the presumption of innocence—which had been on the books for decades but not used since 9/11, was implemented again. Out of 42 Britons with their passports torn up by the Home secretary, 40 were Muslims. It has been assumed that this operation was prompted to please the American wish to threaten their lives or liberty once these Muslims were deprived of their nationality. Governmental efforts are currently made to sanction Britons with single citizenship as well.

DOI: 10.1057/9781137428004.0006

"Clearly, with the London bombings of 2005 in mind, the Commons is still acting on fears that Muslims who might be radicalized abroad will return home to threaten the British isles" (Stafford Smith, 2014). By contrast, the American Supreme Court in its 1958 *Trop v. Dulles* decision asserted that depriving people of their citizenship would leave them stateless and that statelessness was a form of punishment "more primitive than torture." Yet the CIA cooperation with the British intelligence on noncitizens makes the latter particular vulnerable. As asked in the debate at the House of Lords in April 2014, is the purpose of enhancing the citizenship-stripping powers ensuring "that we might be able to do things that make people vulnerable and deny them their rights, creating yet more black holes where no law obtains?" (*Ibid.*)

In 2007, 84% of Muslims affirmed being treated fairly by British society (Mirza et al., 2007) and as elsewhere, they claimed their loyalty to institutions. This may change in the future if antiterrorist policies harden and if fairness and signs of inclusion of Muslims in British society are not strengthened.

New York

After the attacks of 9/11, the precautionary principle went gradually into effect. Neighborhoods' safety against a range of risks and threats became an important priority in New York City because of the vulnerability of its dense population and of its global political, economic, and cultural assets.[5]

The city decided to give itself adequate policing tools to protect it from terrorist threats. A Real Time Crime Centre was created at One Police Plaza, in order to store numbers, maps, diagrams, and huge data files. Policemen on the streets were given Blackberries to report crimes which would be immediately processed by the central computer. Police officers from the Emergency Service Unit, heavily armed, walked in public spaces (as officers do in the French Vigipirate Program). Their goal was to check places which could be potential targets but the aim was also to make the police visible to serve as a reminder that the city was vulnerable as 9/11 had tragically shown. A number of NYPD police officers were required to speak foreign languages and dialects in order to understand what a foreign suspect told them and to enable informers and undercover officers to infiltrate immigrant communities. Dozens of officers, fluent in Arabic, Bengali, or Farsi, were recruited from immigrant groups for this purpose. Only by cooperating with immigrant

DOI: 10.1057/9781137428004.0006

communities might information begin to trickle upward and for such reason, the NYPD always refused to cooperate with the Immigration Services and give them names of undocumented immigrants (except for those in prison). Local law enforcers need to talk to moderate as well as to radical community and religious leaders, use cameras and other technical resources, and rely on their know-how to be more efficient. Searching a suspect building or observing street action may lead to confrontation with youth gangs, drug dealers, organized criminals, or potential terrorists. Both intelligent counterterrorism and ward policing need to rely on excellent knowledge of the streets and their social environments. Local expertise and new technologies are complementary, even if numerous local measures arguably aim at soothing public opinion rather than at impeding further attack. The issue, then, is communication—between police patrols operating at street level, intelligence services using surveillance techniques, Internet analysts, terrorist judges, and other actors. It implies renouncing a top-down approach as the sole means of transmission of knowledge and opting, instead, for partnerships.

From the residents' perspective however, being protected by the police entails costs. Risk management and the surveillance of public spaces imply endless searches; inside private buildings, it is no longer possible to enter without showing some form of IDs. In better equipped centers, magnetic and biometric screens, or facial identification cameras allow to check who gets in and out of a building and to deny entry to unknown faces. In poorer areas, the police patrols are required to act as a safety net for the mainstream society, making sure that everyone is where they belong. Location matters. Tracing risk residents' mobility from one allocated space to another is one of the tasks of street police patrols.

Sociologist Marcuse denounces the "barricading" and "citadelization" of the city (2002: 599) and rightly denounces the correlation of risk to the very idea of the city. The rise of electronic surveillance and the virtual space of databases lead, indeed, to a reconfiguration and to a re-territorialization of urban order.

Concerning Muslims in the context of post-9/11, the belligerent rhetoric used by the Homeland Security Administration addressed not only territorial security but the political and cultural community one belongs to, in an approach of inclusion/exclusion. Many usual Muslim visitors, businessmen, scholars, students to the US became reluctant to visit the country, due to hassles with visas, controls, and unfriendly remarks. This is the case for many moderate Muslims.

DOI: 10.1057/9781137428004.0006

Some conservative media developed the idea of a silent and infiltrated fifth column correlated to Arab-Muslim populations in the post-9/11 imaginary, despite the fact that Arabs in America are part of the middle classes, two thirds of them Christians, a third Muslim and African-American, and most of the two other thirds affluent immigrants. A vast majority of them disapproved strongly of these attacks. Identifying the profile of who should be under reasonable suspicion among this heterogeneous group changed the criteria of inclusion and of exclusion within the American nation. Before September 11, suspects for the American police were—and are still—visible historical minorities, black and Latino young males. A large number of them were incarcerated in the 1980s and 1990s, especially if they were gang members, dealing drugs, or committing violent assaults. After 9/11, male immigrants from the Middle East, under 35 years old, or hyphenated Americans from Arab-Muslim countries, were suspected of being disloyal or leading a double life. They were put under surveillance and detained whenever they were poorly protected by legal services. Most of them had only violated immigration laws, were arrested in the follow-up of 9/11, some of them convicted, others incarcerated without due process of law. Preventing violent acts via incarceration, in fact, hardly reduced crime and did not alleviate fear of crime.

Ten years after 9/11, a Gallup poll revealed that almost half of Muslim Americans (they are 2.6 million in the US) experienced religious or racial discrimination in 2010 (Goodstein, 2011). This was higher than for members of any other religious group. Yet as a religious minority, they were neither alienated nor disaffected; they expressed confidence in the fairness of elections and 60% of them said that they trusted the FBI (vs. 75% of other religious groups who did trust the FBI). On the whole, they were optimistic about the future, as loyal Americans, a finding also encountered in France and in Britain.

In a new development, following the election of Mayor de Biaso and the appointment of W. Bratton as police chief, the NYPD abandoned its secretive program, consisting of dispatching plainclothes detectives in Muslim neighborhoods to eavesdrop on conversations and build files on residents, infiltrate Muslim student groups on college campuses, and keep information on participants to specific lectures. Around mosques, they collected license plate numbers of cars in parking lots and videotaped worshippers. Civil rights groups such as the Arab American Association of New York criticized a program sowing mistrust for law enforcement in Muslim communities. The Demographic Unit, as it was

DOI: 10.1057/9781137428004.0006

first called before being renamed the Zone Assessment Unit, had become less active since the change of mayoralty. The Unit had never been able to collect any leads (Apuzzo and Goldstein, 2014). Will this spying strategy really stop or will the police be satisfied with suppressing the name of a controversial unit? This case reveals the efficiency of pressure groups in defense of immigrants' rights who may be heard at the right time, due to new circumstances.

This example shows the distinction which remains between African-Americans who came to the US involuntarily as slaves and have been continuously apprehended with suspicion by the police regardless of their class/social status (one remembers the Harvard Professor Henry Gates' arrest) and immigrants who voluntarily came to settle in the country, and who despite hard times, maintain their trust in institutions. Should such generalization be analyzed according to class, gender, age, and location as it should in a larger research, they would obviously reveal major differences in attitudes and perceptions of the police among them.

Is community policing the right approach?

Debates relative to the methods, value, and diversity of community policing have been numerous in the past 20 years; yet, due to the segmentation of disciplines, there are relatively few comparative studies on policing, race/ethnicity, space, and the management of social order. Despite the pitfalls that authors of comparative research experience, such studies are worth pursuing. Not only should they be cross-national, whenever possible, but changes, divergences, variations, and evolutions within countries should be emphasized. Just as communities are a complex phenomenon, indeed, with wide divergences in their definition, community policing also changes, sometimes introduced as a problem-solving strategy. A distinction should be emphasized between what is defined as "community policing" (definitely linked to modes of policing in some countries) and the "policing of communities" in very diverse cities (Body-Gendrot, 2011).

How can police work be better accepted by inner-city residents? Can interactions be improved by modes of policing closer to residents? It has been hinted at in previous chapters that on such orientation, opinions diverge according to countries.

France

When wondering whether institutional procedures and outcomes by the police are fair and generate consent in France, one should point out that most members of the public do not have direct contact with the police and that the experience of those who have varies not only between individuals but also for those who have had more than one encounter of this type. In polls, a large majority of the French have positive views of the police (83% in a Sofres poll of 2004 and 75% in a BVA poll in 2012). In 2008, the police force was the best rated public service (67% vs. 46% for justice). In one of the few studies involving a sample of the French adult population and a sample of the "new" French population, the two samples shared the same level of confidence in the judiciary (respectively 61% and 62%) but for the police, they differed (respectively 77% and 58%). It is also among the sample of "new" French that the highest percentage of those "not trusting the police at all" was found (20% vs. 8% for the general population) after controlling for age, education, SES, and political orientation (Brouard and Tiberj, 2005). If too few signals of institutional legitimacy are sent to these "new" French citizens from inner cities, it follows that police presence is perceived as illegitimate.

Still, these findings are somewhat puzzling, since the French national police holds no accountability to citizens. Whether the weight of the French state grants legitimacy to the institution or cultural parameters enter the explanation, this needs further development. The police benefit from an "inferred" legitimacy granted to the state the sovereign domain of which includes security, and to public services supported by three out of four French.

As in other countries, problems of police legitimacy come from "interactions among police culture and structure, overrepresentation among offenders of members of some minority groups, young men's high levels of testosterone and cultural differences" (Tonry, 2008: 6). In countries like the UK and the US, ethnic and racial statistics are used by pressure groups to require institutions to redress discrimination and ethnic profiling, and to provide transparency on police work. In France, the debate over ethnic statistics still divides social scientists and political elites.

Neighborhood policing or "proximity policing" or "policing by consent" models have never been popular among French police forces and their unions. There is hardly any relationship between the officers and the districts in which they work. They are recruited from throughout the country and assigned according to needs. Many spend the better part of their careers attempting to return to their own region, through a series of transfers (Zauberman and Levy, 2003). The idea of police

DOI: 10.1057/9781137428004.0006

officers having ties to the place where they work goes against the concept of a public service for all.

In 2002, Sarkozy dismantled this policing approach launched by the Left in 1997 and enforced in 1999. Although it was difficult to evaluate a reform after only three years, police unions and a majority of those representing precinct commanders claimed that they never had enough resources to organize meetings with populations and to clarify crimes (the rates of successful investigation of crimes were under 9% for all crimes and 5% for street crimes in Paris, in 1995). Nicolas Couteau, then the head of the General Union of the police, complained that community policing missions were unclear: "too often a policeman is meant to be a therapist, a psychologist or a social worker." Another union leader added that "the contact with the populations does not consist of organizing soccer games.... We are not here to meet social goals (*faire du social*)" (Ceaux and Smolar, 2003). As in the US, a majority of policemen shared the idea that community policing was not real police work, that they had nothing to learn from populations whose expectations were too diverse and incoherent. Moreover, since policemen on the field could report more crimes, figures of delinquency were rising and it was politically costly. In brief, precinct commanders argued that they preferred to receive clear-cut orders from their hierarchy rather than meeting the blurred and ambiguous demands from populations. There was also a deeper fear, that of balkanization, of becoming accountable to politically diversified mayors, some of them under pressure from politicized and organized groups, whereas the police' shared motto was that citizens should never be partners of policemen, even less their advisors (Mouhanna, 2008: 78).

Another characteristic of the French police making this reform impossible is the "fortress" mentality inherited from a specific culture. Numerous policemen regarding themselves as "serious family men," note that, in the deprived neighborhoods, they feel despised by the populations who spit on them, stone their cars, insult them—all this within a general indifference from mainstream society. In the interviews that we carried out, they claimed that their isolation from the outside world is their mode of protection. Numerous policemen feel "harassed" by people, the media, politicians, or their own hierarchy. Policemen resent the state that does not grant them enough recognition and pays them poorly; they resent Parliament members passing laws which are lenient for the delinquents; they resent justice and judges accused to be "soft"; they resent those youths that they find more and more violent, and less and less law-abiding (Ceaux

DOI: 10.1057/9781137428004.0006

and Smolar, 2003). They feel instrumentalized by the political sphere. A few years ago, organizational problems of a public sector under pressure were emphasized, due to the lack of resources and a loss of confidence in assigned missions, values, and identity. Too much significance seemed to be given to the internal management rather than to the missions of public service; too much pressure put on young policemen contributed to the exacerbation of tensions, especially those related to the ownership of public space (Body-Gendrot, 2009). Confronted by residents reproaching them for being invisible or too visible, inefficient or too bothersome, under surveillance and suspected by poor foreign families for all kinds of reasons, policemen responded by suspicion and bitterness, stressing the "dirty hands" problem that policemen complain about. Dominique Duprez and Michel Kokoreff, in their work on drugs, quote a rank-and-file policeman patrolling a public housing project at the periphery of Lille: "Each time we arrest a youth from B., there will be problems. Some time ago, after we stopped one at the student dormitory his friends told us: 'If you don't let him go, we will harass you all night long.' This is what happened, they torched cars all night long" (2000: 276).

The rhetoric relative to fear of crime tends to turn policemen into the wardens of Republican order. It raises disproportionate expectations in comparison with the resources and the training they have received. The youngest policemen, assigned to the most difficult neighborhoods, are not prepared to confront unexpected problems. This explains the mutual misunderstandings between them (aiming to restore order, arrest troublemakers, and be respected for that role) and the residents in problem areas (who have diversified attitudes, some of them encouraging policemen when they stop troublemakers, others expressing their outrage, while most remain indifferent) (Body-Gendrot, 2009: 670). Under such conditions, it is not surprising that many policemen would be hostile to community policing.

The composition of the police

The policemen that we interviewed at the CNDS (Police Appeals Commission) regularly denied ethnic profiling and stated that the youths that they controlled are French, and that the color of the skin makes no difference. When asked to open its ranks to second- and third-generation immigrants, the national police institution however has opted for assigning this task to private security agencies and to municipal local forces. An unofficial number estimated the number of rank-and-file minority policemen to less than 9% in 2012. In terms of careers, French constables start at a low monthly salary (health and pension benefits being taken care of) around age 23 (vs. around 28 in Britain) and even though they have more diplomas than in the past, their career follows that of civil servants with slow promotions. Unlike American police officers who can get easily promoted if they are efficacious, such is rarely the case with the status of the French public functionary. Thus, it is understandable that, when assigned to marginalized areas to arrest petty delinquents, French policemen have the feeling that they do "a dirty job" and they ask for transfer as soon as they arrive. Police recruits are almost never selected from problem communities such as the high-risk urban zones; 90% of them coming from provincial localities are sent to the Parisian problem districts as their first position. They are influenced by what they see continuously on television and are not familiar with the urban culture of the high-risk zones. It is difficult for them to distinguish among youths all dressed, more or less, the same, with hoods and the rappers' paraphernalia, and to isolate real offenders (Bellot, Thibau, 2008). Only 10% of the recruits in police academies come from the Parisian region; 90–95% of first jobs after the academy are located in this region (Bonnet and Zagrodski, 2012). In 2007, an 86% turnover of police chiefs—not to mention the rank and file—was observed in Seine-Saint Denis, the most sensitive area in France. Before 1941, when the police were decentralized and recruits came from within the locality they policed, policemen were then recruited locally and accountable to local populations and to their political representatives. But the downside of this system was that they were also accused of corruption and clientelism (Body-Gendrot, 2009).

In decentralized countries, police reforms are frequently triggered by pressures exerted by organized minority groups acting from the bottom-up, by legitimized antidiscriminatory organizations which, under favorable circumstances, find political allies in the system of decision-making or by official reports after a serious event involving the police. But in France, the national police is insulated from third-party advocates whose issues are not taken up by mainstream political parties whether from the Left or from the Right.

Britain

Since the end of the 1990s, community initiatives have had an impact on modes of policing in Britain. The more extensive the local autonomy, the more citizens expect accountability from the police. If the latter fails in their maintenance of social order, they are expected to resign.

Public confidence has long been a policy aim in Britain. The "reassuring police" form it has taken is combined with a service-oriented approach as a means of restoring "public confidence," what Rittel and Webber (1973) have labeled a "wicked issue," complicated, demanding, defying simple solutions. While one can understand that what the public thinks, feels, and says about the police serve the interest of the state which may be perceived by citizens as fulfilling its side of the social contract what is more challenging is letting citizens in the name of public interest occupy the center stage. According to the words of Her Majesty's Inspectorate of Constabulary:

We have adopted an "outside-in" approach, as opposed to the "inside-in" of the past. By "outside-in" I mean putting the public centre-stage. We start with *their* questions, their understanding, and *their* concerns (original emphasis) (O'Connor, 2010).

What is the meaning of "public" in light of multicultural, multiplural-ist, and consumer-oriented societies? How the police is multi-agency policing to reassure distinct publics, reach silent constituencies generate both expectations and satisfactory results?

Take London as an example. The world-city has been widely increasing in size and ethnic and racial heterogeneity in the last 20 years, and is expected to continue to do so. Some neighborhoods mix a wide variety of ethnicities, religions, classes, and ages. The Metropolitan Police Service operates in 32 wards. Drawing on the experience of the Chicago Alternative Policing Strategy (Skogan and Harnett, 1997), emphasizing beat police, consultation with residents and visibility on the streets, the reform of the reassuring police initiated by Blair emphasizes policing by "active cooperation" with community residents (Innes, 2004; 2007). This form of neighborhood policing's challenge has then been to meet the needs of very diverse areas, and of the very different people who live within them. A focus on locally identified priorities became a major emphasis for this policy with the development of Citizen-Focused Policing. Regular meetings have been arranged to meet the local police teams (Millie, 2010: 226). The police report card scheme measures the police force performance in the neighborhoods, according to their visible presence, their responses to matters of concerns to the residents, their points of reference on the street, and the reassurance that they generate.

DOI: 10.1057/9781137428004.0006

In the annual Home Office surveys (2005), individual perception of their local area differs. Attitudes toward police and policing are seen as more influenced by individual characteristics than by the neighborhoods where they live. Perceptions are diverse. Some people may be reassured by seeing numerous policemen on the street, while others are confused, anxious, or irritated. Such issues also concern those who are being reassured. Some people may be happy to be consulted on police performances, the "worried well," but others may distrust the force or remain indifferent. Risk populations such as young minorities or other "usual suspects" may not be reassured.

There seems to be a lot of demagoguery in the approach consisting of meeting any public expectation. In 2004, Prime Minister Blair already stated that "we want to revive the idea of community policing, but for a modern world.... And we will give local communities a real say in deciding the priorities for the new neighborhood policing teams" (Home Office, 2004). In 2010 the conservative manifesto pursued that line: "we will give people the information they need to challenge their neighborhood police teams to cut crime" (Conservative Manifesto, 2010). Research addressing the way the police and local communities view and understand each other in two English localities shows that letting the public set police priorities may be too much of a challenge for the police (Westmarland, 2010). In the eyes of the latter, they are not a business catering to customers. As long as there is a consensus to be shared, police as partners in minimizing harm is the key aim, but in case of challenges, the police should have the last word. In comparison with France, English police officers have a greater sense of serving the community and supporting victims. In terms of essential tools regarding the police officer's relationship with the public, one can contrast the "French firearm" versus the "English tongue" (Cassan, 2010).

Concerning the composition of the British police, it appears that the use of ethnic and racial categories regarding communities does not make societies free of racial bias. Years after the MacPherson report, and due to the politicization of Muslim identity and its impact on policing, numerous measures have proven more symbolic than efficient. An IPCC survey found that almost a third of all Asian respondents fear being subjected to police harassment if they issue a complaint against their force. The IPCC has been criticized for "failing minority victims" (Chakraborti, 2007: 121–122). The recruitment of a more ethnically diverse police workforce has stalled because of a failure to get across the business and operational case for diversity. Minorities in the British police (3%) do not match their proportion in the population (6%), all the more so in the higher ranks. The process of consultation with all sections of communities has been too frequently dominated by police-led agendas, especially after terrorist attacks and the questioning of the representativeness of Muslim leaders' views. Public confidence in what the police does is not derived from minority representation but from the quality of the service and interaction with citizens.

The United States

After the race riots of the 1960s, several commission reports advocated changes in its mode of policing in inner cities. The issue at stake here was how to obtain consent and from whom, in particular from disaffiliated minorities resenting the police more than other components of the population. Should authorities command them through their control, exert force, and carry firearms since so many residents did? For African-American sociologist Anderson (1999) beyond the cost in human capital associated with tough policies of control, another cost, less often perceived, has to do with the growing illegitimacy of laws and institutions in the eyes not only of those arrested but of those of law abiders from their community as well. There is a feeling of unfairness felt by all residents, in terms of legal processes and outcomes, and the citizens' level of commitment to compliance weakens. In the minority community studied by Anderson, the consequence is that adults interested in transmitting law-abiding norms to youths eventually lose in their competition with teen peer-groups. When there are too few positive signals of government legitimacy within a group to support compliance, the peer groups supporting law-breaking wins (Fagan and Meares, 2008).

Should, then, citizens be part of the production of social order and should they coproduce security along with law enforcers servicing them? This is what local governments and cities perturbed by the race riots required, they asked for community policing.

Regarding the police instead of a "fortress-like mentality," the American police see themselves as a thin blue wall and, in the inner cities, they tend to oppose deserving working poor to undeserving ones (Bonnet and Zagrodski, 2014). Compared with the French national organization of the police, what prevails is decentralization. The Mayor and the police chief are accountable. Appointing a black person at the head of the LAPD after the riots of 1992 changed the image of the institution in

DOI: 10.1057/9781137428004.0006

minorities' eyes whereas the appointment of the Police Prefect in Paris is hardly noticed by public opinion. French precinct commanders belong to the public service; they are protected by its rules and have a life-long job. Such is not the case in the US. When Bratton was appointed police chief by Mayor Giuliani, three precinct commanders out of four were fired and replaced by younger, more flexible recruits. Those who were fired looked for police jobs in another city where police recruiting is done locally. Many of them did, with a promotion in the city where they moved. Once community policing is defined as a priority, it would be precarious for precinct chiefs under the supervision of the police chief to oppose it.

The composition of the police

After the *Equal Employment Opportunity Act* was passed in 1972, more minority officers were indeed hired. Actually, between 1970 and 2008, their numbers doubled. In the 62 largest police departments, they comprise 38% of the 62 largest police departments. The presence of minorities in a local police force reflects the racial composition of a city. For instance, Detroit which is three quarters minority populated has a 63% minority police force.

Minority officers appeared in the local police forces at the end of the 19th century and it would take a number of years before they would be promoted sergeants. Black mayors started appointing minority police chiefs in the 1970s in Cleveland, Newark, Atlanta, Washington DC, followed by Chicago, New York City, Houston a few years later. Because of black- on-black violence and crime, often in their communities, black police officers were assigned patrols in ghettoized areas where the drug trade, weapons, and gangs caused trouble for the residents. In 2007, 67% of policemen were required to wear protective body armor at all times (59% in 2003) and 61% to have video cameras in their patrol cars. In Rialto in California in 2013, a majority of police officers carried cameras on their uniforms. It is said that, following that reform, the use of force fell 66% and the number of complaints against the police force has dropped by 88% but this data is to be considered cautiously. In this city, the homicide rate was 17 per 100,000 in 2002, it has dropped to 7.7 per 100,000 in 2011, that is, around 300 murders. When, after New York, he became Police chief, Bratton eased relations between minorities and the LAPD with a new community policing approach (Zagrovski, 2014).

DOI: 10.1057/9781137428004.0006

On the whole, community policing is not the most frequent approach among the local police forces. Formerly associated with political machines marked by corruption, it found a revival with the broken windows hypothesis and it was chosen here and there to discard problems associated with a professional police force cut from the residents. Its function of protection and the discretion left on the field to policemen having to act very rapidly accompanied a need to get rid of incivilities and to secure neighborhoods. This approach worked better in middle-class areas. In high-crime areas, policemen were busy tackling serious crimes. Safety sometimes went along with care providing, as in San Diego. But populations and neighborhoods are not homogeneous and community policing is more easily done in safe places. It does not contribute to the reduction of crime; its function is symbolic, showing that the institution is proactive. It will not bring an efficient regulation of behaviors but in policing appearances, it will give the impression that it tries to do so.

To summarize, on the whole, it is unhelpful and unrealistic to demand perfect police; instead we should aim to achieve "good enough" policing, reevaluating and questioning the concepts of fairness and effectiveness (Bowling, 2007: 17). Variations come from culture, styles of policing, majority and minority groups' views, perceived legitimacy of state institutions and of processes in the eyes of the public at large, and in those with direct dealings with the police.

The divergences come also from the numerous variations taken by forms of inner cities and their evolution. A fundamental difference between the various police forces studied here comes from degrees of centralization and decentralization among the forces and from their forms of recruiting, and accountability. It ensues that the relationship between police and citizens may not be based uniquely on rewards or on threats but also on concepts or trust inherited from the past. Another important factor of differentiation is linked to the relationship citizens have with their institutions, referring to the range of local autonomy and to the centrality of the notion of *community* in a culture.

Police styles remain very different: French police officers favor, respectively, distrust and anonymity in their relationships with citizens, and distance and relative indifference toward victims. In contrast, English police officers display a greater sense of serving the community.

And yet, does it make such a difference? Ensuring that equal proportions of different social groups are punished is not the goal of the criminal justice system, as remarked by Smith (1994). The legitimacy and fairness of the French system does not seem more questionable than it is in Britain (Anderson, 2011). What is "effective enough" or "fair enough" may differ from community to community.

European Courts and treaties' approaches

In Europe, several cases have been brought before the European Court of Human Rights (ECHR) and French courts with regard to abuse by the French police. It appears that antidiscrimination policies or court decisions have had little influence in France. However, since 1997, a large set of treaties and laws are existing to fight against discriminations. The Amsterdam treaty of 1997, in its article 13, defined all of the discriminations that could be sanctioned. A European directive against racial discriminations, "race," adopted in 2000 imposed upon the member states of the EU to respect the equality of treatment without any distinction of race or ethnic origin. Following the directive, the topic of "equal opportunities" has been put on the European political agenda as a priority in 2007. Ethnic or racial origins are the most frequent criteria of discrimination in Europe.

Notes

1   This part borrows in part from Body-Gendrot (2012: 71–74).
2   This section borrows from Body-Gendrot (2012: ch. 2).
    bodygendrot/?K=9780230284210, Copyright.
3   This part borrows from Body-Gendrot (2012: 95 and sq.).
4   This section borrows from Body-Gendrot (2012: ch. 3).
5   This part borrows in part from Body-Gendrot (2012: 77–78, 80–82).

5

Conclusion

Abstract: *Our research shows that policing by "consent," based on trust, as advocated in Britain and in the US, is efficient for the management of daily life in inner cities. The French model of policing, based on order maintenance appears more efficient at first sight to check disturbances in inner cities. Yet, on the whole, modes of policing in the three countries express commonalities and although repression is accepted, the public will not tolerate police abuse. Reforms have then been advocated supported by research and human rights groups. Nevertheless, reconciling knowledge and police practices remains arduous. Finally, making their environment more inclusive is a sound approach for cities. Citizens are not merely passive, they can resolve low-intensity conflicts. Good local governance, better channels of expression and of representation for disaffiliated residents can alleviate the urgency for social protest.*

Body-Gendrot, Sophie and Catherine Wihtol de Wenden,. *Policing the Inner City in France, Britain, and the US.* New York: Palgrave Macmillan, 2014. DOI: 10.1057/9781137428004.0007.

Our research has attempted to discover how a system of social order in contemporary multicultural societies can function and, in doing so, uncover "surprising differences and unexpected similarities" (Nelken, 2010). To this end, at the local level and depending on the countries' institutions, efficient actors can be mobilized such as police reformers, immigrants and minority organizations, local authorities, architects and urban designers, social services and residents, and at the national level, lawmakers, judges, pressure groups, and the media.

Trust in the police

The issue of trust, allowing the police to achieve their goals more efficiently in inner cities divides Britain and the US on one hand and France on the other. It is a shared idea in Britain and the US that policing by "consent" entails the cooperation of citizens (Tyler, 1990). Importance is given to police leadership, legitimacy, trust, and to the respect of procedural rules, and consequently, to the nature of the relations that the police have with the population among in which they intervene. Fairness includes "openness and transparency, the capacity to listen to what people treated as suspects have to say, avoiding embarrassing them, allowing people—whether they are victims, witnesses, suspects, or arrestees—to give their version of the facts and to answer their questions" (Bowling, 2007: 28). The Beetham model (1991), according to which the governed give "consent" to authorities to exercise their power if they do it in a way consistent with their moral beliefs, theoretically (or ideally) prevails in Britain and the US General interest results from a bargaining among various interest groups resulting in negotiations and, at the end, in a compromise after which common interest reaches a consensus for the best of all. Such a model appears to be successful in inner cities' daily life with multicultural settings. Surveys from the Home Office in Britain or from various Foundations in the US demonstrate that a "reassuring police" or an integrated police force in interaction with neighborhood' residents, acting as consultants, is appreciated in a majority of places that are not antagonistic to police and to institutions.

Whereas the British and the American perspectives consider the police as a corps meeting civil society's demands for protection and security, by contrast, in France, the police is a body created by the political power the mission of which is to impose law enforcement and social discipline to lower classes and marginal organizations, according to a Weberian model (1922/1968). This implies that a centralized authority to which policemen are accountable controls a national police of 260,000 policemen and gendarmes recruited nationwide. General interest is provided by the state. It is taken for granted that citizens are expected to obey the law and policemen to follow the rules. It implies that policemen look at themselves as professional outsiders, even more so if they belong to the anti-squad forces (CRS and BAC). They have no knowledge of the context in which they operate. Negotiation, mediation, and prevention are alien, or some might say, forbidden practices (Mouhanna, 2008: 84).

That cooperation is not searched for by the French police does not imply that they are not respected by the public or that they are inefficient. Not enough research has been carried out regarding this refusal of "consent," except when community policing was rejected by police unions. Research has shown that concern with proximity between police and the populations is only meaningful if police are not only serving the state but are also accountable for their outcomes. Accountability does not belong to the French institutional culture. The top management of the police under pressure from political elites requires results and efficiency from the police. French citizens (paying taxes is enough for them) are not co-producing services and institutions are not asked to be accountable.

This model could be criticized from the Anglo-American viewpoint if it did not prove its efficiency when dealing with order maintenance. It seems to us that there is an incompatibility in pursuing the two missions: that of policing by consent and reassurance in a friendly environment and that of suppression of disorders (confrontations, traffics, ambushes, etc.) provoked by rebellious rebellious inner city youths.

Repression

On the field, despite these different doctrines, when disorders occur in inner cities or elsewhere in the city, the police forces of the three countries resort to repressive methods that look strangely similar. They operate through sophisticated weaponry, with officers equipped with riot-gear and trained in riot-control tactics such as "trudge and wedge" and "kettling"—that is, pushing against a resisting crowd with synchronized movements, thus, maximizing physical force (Waddington and

DOI: 10.1057/9781137428004.0007

Wright, 2008; Body-Gendrot, 2014, in press). Strategies of incapacitation based on risk management make use of metal barricades around contested terrains, restricting movements from the sidewalks and access to zones of contention. Depending on context, police may make use of water canons and horses to disperse crowds. Surveillance, identification, and control are facilitated by flood lights, CCTV infrastructure, and various surveillance vehicles (Body-Gendrot, 2014, in press). During disorderly events, undercover and infiltrated officers gather intelligence, transfer photos and videos to analysts who subsequently use huge data files to establish profiles of the participants. Security policies are also increased via zoning and walls proliferation, sometimes at the demand of the police, as in New York.

The role of the police as a brake to public disorder is, thus, established and legitimized by the support that the public gives them for bringing back the efficient return to order. However, although the police are authorized to use diverse means, in more or less controlled ways, to re-establish order, in European countries at least, the growing aversion to open acts of violence by the police has made police abuse unacceptable (Body-Gendrot, 2014, in press). The creation of various forms of control on police behavior (Police Complaints Commissions, Human Rights organizations, internal police surveillance corps) shows that policemen avoid being sanctioned and exposed to public opinion's verdicts.

Police reforms

Are police reforms efficient? Recent research has revealed a certain amount of evidence (Sherman and Neyroud, 2012). The classical opposition in criminology is between two options: heightened security in places or neutralizing risk people; containing offenders in their sensitive neighborhoods or tracking and checking them when they move to more collective spaces like sport stadiums or leisure places.

Concerning the inner cities, research shows, indeed, that crime is concentrated in very small geographic units of analysis where the police should focus their main resources and problem-solving efforts. Police should concentrate their investigative energies on the small group of offenders committing the most serious crimes in view of the greatest common good rather than pursuing the vast majority of offenders presenting a low risk of harm. Restorative research shows that a good

DOI: 10.1057/9781137428004.0007

strategy whereby offenders are expected to apologize to their victims should concentrate on those with a risk of multiple victimizations. Face-to-face meetings with offenders reduce a feeling of retaliation. Finally, on the difficult topic of legitimacy, scholars state that attention paid to procedures can help the police identify behavior, tactics, and strategies that many members of minority communities find problematic, leading to disaffection, even though the behaviors, tactics, and strategies may seem lawful and, when considered in isolation, effective. In some environments, the delivery of fairness in policing may be problematic. As observed by a police captain in New York accused of racial bias: "90% of the neighbourhood is black, so, yes, the police arrest black people" (he himself is an African-American (Bonnet, Zagrodski, 2013). Police culture comprises "'dictionaries" of types of people with whom the police come into contact, "directories" of general approaches to police work, and "recipes" for action in specific situations (Chan, 1997). It is important not to neglect the psychological aspects of legitimacy in individual encounters— what we called earlier "the offender and the officer variables." The issue of respect, shown or not, by the police was recurrent in our own interviews with minorities. Finally, there may be moments when maintaining public order requires the nonenforcement of the law, for instance when thugs infiltrate students' demonstrations and all the groups are dressed alike.

The Scottish Institute for Policing Research (Lum, 2011) confirms such findings: 79% of successful interventions studied occur at "micro-places" or "neighborhoods.". Sixty-four percent of them are "focused" or tailored strategies. Eighty percent of them are either "proactive" or highly proactive."

What does not work is also well-known: sending young policemen as their first job to inner cities and for too little time; applying arbitrary rules with conformity and no sense of flexible adjustment, according to the environment.

Due to such knowledge, it is urgent to reconcile police practices and knowledge. This is, unfortunately, not the case and resistance to change is strong within police institutions.

Lastly, too few reforms address racism, discrimination, police "canteen" culture, police abuse, and their possible correlation with unrest in inner cities (Waddington, 1999). Policemen training and police management remain sensitive issues and proof of their efficiency are is questionable or related to specific circumstances prohibiting generalizations. If discretion is seen as pragmatic improvisation in response to problem encounters,

DOI: 10.1057/9781137428004.0007

then experience and judgment may come before rules and procedures. Experienced police officers practice selective enforcement and they may choose, in the inner cities, to under-enforce law, as they always have the use of force as a backup if situations call for it.

Changing the composition of the police with the hiring and promotion of more minorities has been efficient at certain times in large American cities. Police unions in France defend the idea of a color-blind Republic, claiming that efficiency in police work is not linked to the composition of the police.

A related issue has to do with promotions for visible minorities inside within the institution. Do policemen with an immigrant or minority background benefit from the same promotion and the same respect as their "white" counterparts? Such does not seem to be the case in France and in Britain, while our research has shown that here and there, minority police chiefs in large American multicultural cities do make a difference.

Minorities' leverage

The politicization of migrations and of Otherness in times of hardship is an obstacle to the progress of rights because specific policies of inclusion trigger a fear of seeing more extreme right votes. This explains why in numerous countries, although they pay taxes, long-term settled immigrant residents are not given voting rights. The issue would extend in the US to the great number of disenfranchised members of minority groups who cannot vote because they have been held in prison at some point in their lifetime.

Our research has shown that in Britain (the Lawrence case) and the US (courts' cases), minorities' organizational capacities have been occasionally successful. They have found allies to defend their causes against discriminatory practices. Places have been open, where those who feel racially or ethnically discriminated against can file a complaint without fearing retaliation. Most police stations in the US have female staffs specifically trained to receive battered women, for instance. In France, since 2005, the creation of antidiscrimination offices with dedicated judges in every court has contributed to show that institutions had a better awareness of the problem. However, currently, this operation has reached its limits. A system of "class actions," as in the US, with collective

DOI: 10.1057/9781137428004.0007

actions led by victims could have more weight. This is under study in France.

Giving a greater visibility to multicultural elites is a strategy that has been successful after 50 years of implementation of policies of affirmative action in the US. These programs were meant to be temporary. Currently, they are threatened as they have created a backlash among excluded white males.

The US is still in a leadership position in promoting minorities' constitutional rights. France still has a long way to go, and Britain, with its "positive actions," is in a medium position.

More inclusive cities

The police cannot solve all of the problems of inner cities. The first on the frontline, cities are forced to be ahead in terms of innovation, prevention, and repair of the social fabric. While reducing inequality and unfairness is not in the cities' grasp, it remains in their power to choose measures and policies at various scales that will alleviate the expulsions of the weakest and allow a diversity of people to live together peacefully with their differences.

Despite different legal traditions, states and cities attempt to be more inclusive by resorting to rules, ordinances, and directives, the goal of which is to protect common values (respect for Human Rights, due process for all, dignity, rule of law, equal treatment, abolition of the death penalty). Governing through security and not through crime is part of the European identity illustrating a "community of feelings" (Girling, 2006). Some cities know how to confront social and civil insecurity with appropriate preventative tools: for example, social mix in multicultural environments can imply quality and affordable housing, density, diversity, and proximity in secure and empowering spaces that benefit every household.

The quality of the environment could allow innovations and incomplete designs. Planners should pay attention to models people have in their minds and create a valorizing and integrative narration for them in the metropolis. People's life opportunities are not determined by the city, but by where they fit into the city and by how they use it. Obviously, living in the inner city limits opportunities, and it is the public domain's responsibility as well as the residents' personal responsibility to alleviate the handicaps cumulating in such spaces.

DOI: 10.1057/9781137428004.0007

The essence of a city is urbanity which can indeed be translated as shared public space where different cultures and classes can meet safely. Under such conditions, hazard, chance, and random encounters with other people may be sources of ideas and innovations. But not everyone is socially mature for such encounters which may also generate fears and insecurity. Various partners in cities, not just the police, have, then, to respond to a wide range of needs with efficiency, discretion, and tolerance.

Diversity and density may, indeed, be sources of conflict in multicultural environments. Frequently, people at the bottom resort to conflict resolution themselves rather than go to the police or to the judge. Some neighborhood watch initiatives may translate, however, into a "NIMBY" (not in my backyard) syndrome. However, patient, modest, almost invisible processes of mediation among diverse, old and new class-differentiated residents and local authorities can also prove efficient (Amin and Thrift, 2002). Providing voices for the different groups that dwell together in the city even without forming a community is an alternative to exclusion and a mode of conflict resolution. The following example shows that both residents and city leaders have a role to play.

Brixton in Britain has a very diversified, multicultural market. Selling products at the market is a first-entry point for immigrants who, then, ferociously defend their turf against newcomers. Recently, West Indians, long settled at the market, were threatened by Eastern Europeans and by Afghans also trying to sell at the market and make a living. Tensions rose. After an incident caused by the theft of an orange by a West Indian and the anger of the Afghan merchant, the latter was stabbed to death by the thief and his friends. The reaction of local authorities, after discussions with the concerned communities, was to hire a policeman speaking pastoun in order to collaborate with Afghan spokesmen and anticipate further trouble. The Afghans were discontent by the fair justice process of Britain which would not immediately have the thief condemned and sent to prison, as would have been the case in their country (Michel, 2015, forthcoming). But this is precisely the reason why mediators and consultative groups within the local police justify their *raison d'être*, reason for existing. Local governance, and channels of expression and of representation can alleviate the urgency for social protest.

The differences revealed here lead to more research allowing to grasp both the macro-mutations taking place and impacting urban space, the expulsions that they generate among nonorganized populations,

DOI: 10.1057/9781137428004.0007

sometimes the local mobilizations denouncing them and the urban management of tensions. It is the duty of cities to prevent and manage unrest, frustrations, violence pertaining to younger generations and, in that respect, "good enough policing" contributes to it.

In the end, this comparative study does not answer all of the questions that it has raised. It aims at starting a debate which has as much to do with police practices, with resilient multicultural cities as with the nature of the state in the three studied countries.

Sophie Body-Gendrot has written the sections relative to Britain and the US, chapters 4 and 5 in the book. Catherine Wihtol de Wenden has written the sections relative to France.

DOI: 10.1057/9781137428004.0007

Bibliography

Abu-Lughod J.2007 *Race, Space, and Riots in Chicago, New York, and Los Angeles,* New York, Oxford University Press.

Amin A. 2003."Unruly Strangers? The 2001 Urban Riots in Britain", *International Journal of Regional and Urban Research,* 27(2), 460–463.

Amin A. and Thrift N. 2002. *Cities: Reimagining the Urban,* Cambridge, Polity Press.

Anderson E. 1999. *Code of the Streets,* New York, Norton.

Anderson E. 2011. *The Cosmopolitan Canopy. Race and Civility in Every Day Life,* New York, Norton.

Anderson M. 2011. *In Thrall to Political Change: Police and Gendarmerie in France,* Oxford, Oxford University Press.

Apuzzo M. and Goldstein J. 2014. "New York drops secret unit that spied on Muslims", *International New York Times,* April 17.

Arslan L. 2011. *Enfants de Marianne et de l'islam,* Paris, Presses Universitaires de France.

Bagguley P. and Hussain T. 2008. *Riotous Citizens: Ethnic Conflict in Multicultural Britain,* Aldershot, Ashgate.

Balibar E. 2005. "La construction du racisme", *Actuel Marx,* 38, 11–28.

Balibar E. and Wallerstein I. 1988. *Race, Nation, Classe. Les identités ambiguës,* Paris, La Découverte.

Bayley D. H. 1994. *Police for the Future,* Oxford, Oxford University Press.

Beetham D. 1991. *The Legitimation of Power,* Atlantic Highlands, NJ: Humanities.

DOI: 10.1057/9781137428004.0008

Bellot M. and Thibau A. 2008. "Police and Discrimination, an Investigation by Radio Program Surpris par la Nuit", *France Culture*, June 25.

Bertho A. 2009. *Le temps des émeutes*, Paris, Bayard.

Bertossi C. and Wihtol de Wenden C. 2007. *Les couleurs du drapeau. L'armée française face aux discriminations*, Paris, Robert Laffont.

Berube M. 2011. The *state of Metropolitan American: Suburbs and the 2010 Census*, Washington, DC, Brookings.

Bittner E. 1974. "Florence Nightingale in the Pursuit of Willie Sutton", in H. Jacob (ed.) *The Potential for Reform of Criminal Justice*, Beverley Hills, Sage, 17–44.

Body-Gendrot S. 1993. *Ville et violence*. Paris, Presses Universitaires de France.

Body-Gendrot S. 1995. "Models of Immigrant Integration in France and in the United States: Signs of Convergence?", in M.P. Smith and J. Feagin (eds) *The Bubbling Cauldron*, Minneapolis, Minnesota Press, 244–262.

Body-Gendrot S. 2000. *The Social Control of Cities?* Oxford, Blackwell. Copyright.

Body-Gendrot S. 2004. "Race, a Word Too Much? The French Dilemma". in M. Bulmer and J. Solomos (eds) *Researching Race and Racism*, London, Routledge, 150–161.

Body-Gendrot S. 2007."Police, Justice and Youth Violence in France", in Tyler T. (ed.) *Legitimacy and the Criminal System. International Perspective*, New York, Russell Sage, 243–276.

Body-Gendrot S. 2008. "Urban 'Riots' in France: Anything New?", in P. Ponsaert (ed.) *Local Security Policy in the Netherlands and Belgium*, Den Haag, Netherlands, Boom Juridische Utig.

Body-Gendrot S. 2010. "Youth, Police, Marginality and Discrimination in the Banlieues of France", *Ethnic and Racial Studies*, 33(4), 656–674.

Body-Gendrot S. 2012. *Globalization, Fear and Insecurity: The Challenges for Cities North and South*. Basingstoke, UK, Palgrave Macmillan.

Body-Gendrot S. 2013. "Urban Violence in France and England: Comparing Paris (2005) and London (2011)", *Policing and Society*, 23(1), 6–25.

Body-Gendrot S. 2015. "Public disorders: Practices and Theory", *Annual Review of Law and Social Sciences*, under press.

Body-Gendrot S. and Savitch H.V. 2012. "Urban Violence in the United States and France: Comparing Los Angeles (1992) and Paris (2005)", in K. Mossberger, S. Clarke, P. Jones (eds) *Oxford Handbook of Urban Politics*. Oxford, Oxford University Press.

DOI: 10.1057/9781137428004.0008

Body-Gendrot S. and Schain M. 1992. "Immigration and Politics: the Case of France and the U.S", in D. Horowitz and G. Noiriel. (eds) *Immigration and Ethnicity in France and the U.S.* New York, NYU Press, 411–438.

Body-Gendrot S. and Spierenburg P. 2007. *Violence in Europe*, New York, Springer.

Body-Gendrot S. and Wihtol de Wenden C. 2003. *Police et discriminations*, Paris, Editions de l'Atelier.

Body-Gendrot S. and Wihtol de Wenden C. 2007. *Sortir des banlieues. Pour en finir avec la tyrannie des territoires.* Paris, Autrement.

Body-Gendrot S., Hough M., Kerezsi K., Levy R. and Snacken S. (eds) 2013. *Routledge Handbook of European Criminology*, Oxford, Routledge.

Bonnet F. and Thery C. 2014. "A Ferguson, un nouveau type d'émeutes raciales se dessine. La légitimité de l'action de la police remise en cause", *Le Monde*, August 24.

Bonnet F. and Zagrodzki M. 2012. Comparer les obstacles à la mise en oeuvre du community policing en France et aux Etats-Unis, unpublished paper, Fall 2012.

Boucher M. 2013. *Casquettes contre képis. Enquête sur la police de rue et l'usage de la force dans les quartiers populaires.* Paris, L'Harmattan

Bourbeau P. 2013. "Politisation et sécuritisation des migrations internationales: une relation à définir", *Critique internationale*, 61(4), 127–145.

Bowling B. 2007. "Fair and Effective Policing Methods: Towards 'Good Enough Policing", *Journal of Scandinavian Studies in Criminology and Crime Prevention*, 8, 17–32.

Braga A. and Weisburd D. 2010. *Policing Problem Places*, New York: Oxford University Press.

Bratton W. and Kobler P. 1998.*Turnaround*, New York, Random House.

Brouard S. and Tiberj V. 2005. *Français comme les autres,* Paris, Presses de Sciences-Po.

Bulmer M. and Solomos J. (eds). 2004. *Researching Race and Racism*, London, Routledge.

Campbell B. 1993. *Goliath: Britain's Dangerous Places,* London: Methuen.

Cantle Report 2001 *Community Cohesion*, London, Home Office, HMSO.

Cassan D. 2010. "Police Socialisation in France and in England: How Do They Stand towards the Community Policing Model?", *Journal of Police Studies* 16(3), 243–259.

Ceaux P. and Smolar P. 2003. "Cette circulaire signée Sarkozy qui désavoue la police de proximité", *Le Monde*, February 19, 7.

DOI: 10.1057/9781137428004.0008

Chakraborti N. 2007. "Policing Muslim Communities", in M. Rowe (ed.) *Policing Beyond MacPherson,* Cullompton, Willan. *op.cit.* 107–128.

Chan J. 1997. *Changing Police Culture: Policing in a Multicultural Society,* Cambridge, Cambridge University Press.

Clark K. 1965. *Dark Ghetto. Dilemmas of Social Power*, New York, HarperTorch.

CNDS Rapport. 2004. Sur la part des discriminations dans les manquements à la déontologie de la sécurité, Paris.

Coaffee J., Murakami Wood D. and Rogers P. 2009. *The Everyday Resilience of the City*, New York, Palgrave Macmillan.

Cole D. 2012. "The American Romance with Guns", *The New York Review of Books,* September 27, 48–51.

Colombani J.-M. 2005. "Aprés le choc", *Le Monde,* November, 29.

Commission nationale consultative des droits de l'homme (CNCDH) 2014. *La lutte contre le racisme, l'antisémitisme et la xénophobie. Année 2013.* Paris, la documentation française.

Crawford A. 2002. "The Politics of Community Safety and Crime Prevention in England and Wales: New Strategies and Developments", in P. Hebberecht, D. Duprez (eds) *The Prevention and Security Policies in Europe*, Brussels, VUB University Press, 51–94.

Crawford A. 2010. "Regulating Civility, Governing Security and Policing (Dis)Order Under Conditions of Uncertainty", in J. Blad, M. Hildebrandt, K. Rozemond, M. Schuilenburg, P. Van Calster (eds) *Governing Security under the Rule of Law,* The Hague, Eleven International, 5–21.

Crawford A. and Traynor P. 2012. "Community-based strategies to early interventions with young people", in P. Hebberecht, E. Baillergeau (eds) *Social Crime Prevention in Late Modern Europe*, Brussels, VUB University Press, 63–102.

Critcher C. and Waddington D. (eds) 1996. *Policing Public Order: Theoretical and Practical Issues,* Avebury, Aldershot.

Denham J. 2001. *Building Cohesive Communities: A Report of the Ministerial Group on Public Order and Community Cohesion,* London, Home Office.

De Rudder V. 1991. "Le racisme dans les relations interethniques" *L'Homme et la Societé 4.*

Dickey C. 2009. *Securing the City. Inside American's Best Counterterror force-the NYPD,* New York, Simon and Schuster.

Dubet F. 2009. *Les places et les chances*, Paris, Robert Laffont.

DOI: 10.1057/9781137428004.0008

Duprez D. and Pinet, M. 2001. "La tradition, un frein à l'intégration. Le cas de la police française", *Cahiers de la sécurité intérieure*, 45, 111–138.

Duprez D. and Kokoreff M. 2000. *Les mondes de la drogue*, Paris, Odile Jacob.

Dworkin R. 1977. *Taking Rights Seriously*, Cambridge, Ma, Harvard University Press.

Ehrenreicht, B. and Muhammad D. 2009. "Les Noirs, premières victimes de la récession",*Courrier International*, September 24.

Elias N. and Dunning E. 1986. *Quest for Excitement: Sport and Leisure in the Civilizing Process*, Oxford, Blackwell.

Elias N. and Scotson J.L. 1995. *The Established and the Outsiders*, Newbury, CA, Sage.

European Commission against Racism and Intolerance (ECRI) 2007. *General Policy Recommendations No. 11 on Combating Racism and Racial Discrimination in Policing*. June 29. Strasbourg, Council of Europe.

Fagan J. 2011. "Indignities of Order Maintenance Policing", memo NYU Straus House workshop.

Fagan J. and Meares T. 2008. "Punishment, Deterrence and Social Control: The Paradox of Punishment in Minority Communities", *Ohio State Journal of Criminal Law*, 6(1), 173–229.

Fassin D. 2013. *Enforcing Order: An Ethnography of Urban Policing*, Boston, Polity Press.

Fassin D. 2014. "Pouvoir discrétionnaire et politiques sécuritaires. Le chèque en gris de l'Etat à la police", *Actes de la recherche en sciences sociales*, Dossier Raison d'Etat, 201–202.

Favell A. 2001. "Integration Policy and Integration Research in Europe: A Review and Critique", in T.A. Aleinikopp, D. Klusymeyer (eds) *Citizenship Today: Global Perspectives and Practices*, Washington DC, Brookings Institute, 2001, 349–399.

Flamm M. 2005. *Law and Order. Street Crime, Civil Unrest, and the Crisis of Liberalism in the 1960s*, New York, NY, Columbia University Press.

Fleming J. 2009. "Community policing: Australia", in J. Fleming, A. Wakefield (eds) *The Sage Dictionary of Policing*, Los Angeles, Sage, 38–39.

FRA. 2009. *EU-MIDIS Technical Report; Methodology, Sampling and Fieldwork*, Brussels, European Union Agency for Fundamental Rights. (http://fra.europa.eu/eu-midis):EU-MIDIS

Frey W. 2011a. *Melting Pot Cities and Suburbs; Racial and Ethnic Change in Metro America in the 2000s*, Washington, DC, Brookings.

Frey W. 2011b. *The State of the Suburbs in 1990*, Washington DC, Brookings.

Fourcaut A. Bellanger E. and Flonneau M. 2007. *Paris/Banlieues: Conflits Et Solidarités*, Saint-Etienne, Creaphis.

Gallup. 2011. www.gallup.com/poll/15156/Americans-prioritize-growing-economy. Accessed March 26, 2013.

Garapon A. 1996. *Le Gardien Des Promesses*, Paris, Odile Jacob.

Garbaye R. 2011. *Emeutes vs Intégration. Comparaisons franco-britannique*, Paris, Presses de Sciences Po.

Garland D. 1999. "The Common Place and the Catastrophic: Interpretations of Crime in Late Modernity", *Theoretical Criminology*, 3(3), 353–364.

Garland D. 2001. *The Culture of Control: Crime and Social Order in Contemporary Society,* Chicago, University of Chicago Press.

Gauthier J. 2001. "Des corps étrange(r)s dans la police? Les policiers minoritaires à Paris et à Berlin", *Sociologie du travail*, 53(4), 460–477.

Gauthier J. 2012. "Générations et frustration: deux pistes d'interprétation du racisme policier", www.contretemps.eu/interventions/générations/-frustration-deux-pistes. Accessed February 26, 2014.

General Direction of the Renseignements généraux, Report, November 23, 2005, in *Le Parisien*, December 7, 2005.

Girling E. 2006. "European Identity, Penal Sensibilities and Communities of Sentiment", in S. Armstrong, L. McAra (eds) *Perspectives on Punishment: The Contours of Control*, Oxford, Oxford University Press, 69–81.

Goodstein L. 2011. "Poll Contradicts many stereotypes on Muslims in the US", *New York Times,* August 3.

Gottfredson M. and Hirshi T. 1990. *A General Theory of Crime*. Stanford, CA: Stanford University Press.

Greer S. 2010. "Anti-Terrorist Laws and the UK 'Suspect Community: A reply to Pantazis and Pemberton", *British Journal of Criminology* 50(6), 1171–1190.

Groupe d'études et de lutte contre les discriminations (GELD) 2001. "La sensibilisation aux discriminations dans la fonction publique: l'enjeu de la formation. L'exemple de la police et de la justice?", *Note du GELD,* 4.

Guillaumin C. 1972. *L'idéologie raciste:genèse et langage actuel*. Paris-La Haye, Mouton.

Guillaumin C. 1994. "Racisme", *Pluriel-Recherches*, 2, 67–70.

Hall S. 1991. "Old and new identities, old and new ethnicities", in A.D. King (ed.) *Culture, Globalization and the World-System*, Basingstoke, Macmillan.

DOI: 10.1057/9781137428004.0008

Harcourt B. 2001. *Illusion of Order:The False Promise of Broken Windows Policing,* Cambridge, Harvard University Press.

Heran F. 2010. *Inégalités et discriminations. Pour un usage critique et responsable de l'outil statistique,* Paris, Rapport INED, February 3.

Home Office. 2004. *Confident Communities in a Secure Britain: the Home Office Strategic Plan 2004-2008 Cm 6287,* London, Home Office.

Home Office. 2005. *Race and the Criminal Justice System: an Overview to the Complete Statistics, 2003-2004.* London, Home Office.

Hough M., Jackson J. and Bradford B. 2013. "Trust in Justice and the legitimacy of legal authorities: topline findings from a European comparative study", in S. Body-Gendrot, M. Hough, K. Kerezsi, R. Levy and S. Snacken (eds) *Routledge Handbook of European Criminology,* Oxford, Routledge, 243-265.

Hunt A. 2014. "Racial divide in US defies easy change", *International New York Times,* August 25.

Innes M. 2004. "Reinventing Tradition? Reassurance, Neighbourhood Security and Policing", *Criminal Justice,* 4(2), 151-171.

Innes M. 2007. "The Reassuring Function", *Policing: A Journal of Strategy and Management,* 1(2), 132-141.

International Crisis Group. 2006. "La France face à ses musulmans: émeutes, jihadisme et dépolitisation", March 9, European report no. 172.

Janowitz M. 1999. "Collective Racial Violence: A Contemporary History", in H.D. Graham and T. Gurr (eds) *Violence in America,* Beverly Hills, Sage.

Jobard F. 2002. *Bavures policières. La force publique et ses usages,* Paris, La Découverte.

Jobard F. 2003a. Research Note: Counting Violence Committed by the Police: Raw Facts and Narratives, *Policing and Society,* 13(4), 423-428.

Jobard F. 2003b. "When Policemen Go to Court. a Study on Outrage, Rebellion and Violence against Policemen", *Policing and Society,* December 13(4), 423-428.

Jobard F. 2008. "Ethnizität und Rassismus in der gesellschaftlichen Konstruktion der gefährlichen Gruppen, Polizeikultur und Praxis in den französischen Voroten", *Schweizerische Zeitschrift fur Soziologie,* 34(2), 261-280.

Jobard F., Lévy R., Lamberth J. and Névanen S. 2012. "Measuring Appearance-Based Discrimination: An Analysis of Identity Checks in Paris", *Population,* 67(3), 349-376.

DOI: 10.1057/9781137428004.0008

Katznelson I. 2005. *When Affirmative Action Was White*, New York, Norton.

Keith M. 1993. *Race, Riots and Policing: Lore and Disorder in a Multi-Racist Society*, London, UCL Press.

Kepel G. 2012. *Banlieues de la République*, Paris, Gallimard.

Kneebone E. 2014. "Ferguson, Mo. Emblematic of Growing Suburban Poverty", *Rethinking the Metropolitan Areas*, Washington, DC, Brookings Institute, August 15.

Lagrange H. 2008. "Emeutes, ségrégation urbaine et aliénation politique", *Revue française de science politique*, 3(58), 377–401.

Lagrange H. 2010. *Le déni des cultures*, Paris, Seuil.

Lagrange H. 2013. *En terre étrangère*, Paris, Seuil.

Lapeyronnie D. 2010. *Le ghetto urbain*, Paris, Robert Laffont.

Lappi-Seppälä T. 2011. "Explaiing imprisonment in Europe", *European Journal of Criminology*, 8(4), 303–328.

Levy R. 1987. *Du suspect au coupable: le travail de police judiciare*, Paris/ Genève, Méridiens.

Lieberson S. and Waters M. 1988. *From Many Strands:Ethnic and Racial Groups in Contemporary America*, New York, Russell Sage.

Lijphart A. 1999. *Patterns of Democracy:Government Forms and Performance in Thirty-Six Countries* London, Yale University Press.

Lipset S.M. 1996. *American Exceptionalism: A Double-Edged Word*, New York, Norton.

Lochak D. 1987. "Réflexions sur la notion de discrimination", *Droit Social*, 11.

Lochak D. 1992 "Discrimination against Foreigners Under the French Law" in D. Horowtiz and G. Noiriel (eds) *Immigrants in Two Democracies:French and American Experiences*, New York, New York University Press, 391–410.

Loveday B. 2011. "Going Local? Direct Election and Future Police Governance in England and Wales. an Evaluation of Current Proposals for Reform of Police Service Delivery and Accountability", Paper presented at the conference *Public security in Europe*, Jagellion University, Cracow, October.

Lowi T. 1979. *The End of Liberalism*, New York, Norton, 2nd print.

Lum C., Koper C.S. and Telep C.W. 2011. The Evidence-Based Policing Matrix. *Journal of Experimental Criminology*, 7(1), 3–26.

Lupton R. and Power A. 2004. *Minority Ethnic Groups in Britain*, London, LSE, Case-Brookings Census Briefs, no. 2.

DOI: 10.1057/9781137428004.0008

MacPherson William of Cluny Sir. 1999. "The Stephen Lawrence inquiry", London, Her Majesty's Stationery Office.

Malik K. 2014. "Britain's Bobbies in the Dock", *International New York Times*, March 19, 7.

Manning P.K. 2005. "The Study of Policing", *Police Quaterly*, 8(1), 23–43.

Marcuse P. 2002. "Urban Form and Globalization after September 11th: The View from New York", *International Journal of Urban and Regional Research*, 26(3), 596–606.

Marshall I. 1997. "Introduction", in Haen Marshall I. (ed.) *Minorities, Migrants and Crime*, Thousand Oaks, Sage, ix-xi.

Marshall I. 2001. "The Criminological Enterprise in Europe and the U.S.: A Contextual Exploration", *European Journal of Criminal Policy and Research*, 9(3), 235–257.

Massey D. and Denton N. 1992. *American Apartheid*, Princeton, Princeton University Press.

Metropolitan Police 2012. 4 Days In August: Strategic Review into the Disorder of August 2011—final report. www.met.police.uk London.

Michel L. 2015. "Des émeutes à la gentrification", *L'esprit des villes*, no. 2, forthcoming.

Millie A. 2010. "Whatever Happened to Reassurance Policing?", *Policing. A Journal of Policy and Practice*, 4(3), 225–232.

Miller J., Bland N. and Quinton P. 2000. *The Impact of Stops and Searches on Crime and the Community*. Police Research Series. Paper 127, London Home Office.

Minces J. 1985. *La génération suivante*, Paris, Seuil.

Molotch H. and McClain N. 2003. "Dealing with Urban Terror", *International Journal of Urban and Regional Research*, 27(3), 679–698.

Monjardet D. and Gorgeon C. 2005. "La culture professionnelle des policiers, une attitude longitudinale", *Les cahiers de la sécurité intérieure*, 56, 291–304.

Mouhanna C. 2008. "Police: de la proximité au maintien de l'ordre généralisé?", in Mucchielli L. (ed.) *La Frénésie sécuritaire*, Paris, La Découverte, 77–87.

Mirza M., Senthilkumaran A. and Ja'far Z. 2007. *Living Apart Together: British Muslims and the Paradox of Multiculturalism*, Policy Exchange Report.

National Advisory Commission on Civil Disorders. 1968. The Kerner Commission. *Final Report*. Washington DC, US Government Printing Office, March 1.

DOI: 10.1057/9781137428004.0008

National Commission on the Causes and Prevention of Violence. 1969. The Eisenhower Commission. *To Establish Justice, To Ensure Domestic Tranquility. Final Report*. Washington DC, US Government Printing Office.

Nelken D. 2010. *Comparative Criminal Justice*, Los Angeles, Sage.

Neustadt R. 1960. *Presidential Power*, New York, Mentor.

Newman O. 1973. *Defensible Spaces: People and Design in the Violent City*, London, Architectural Press.

Nocera J. 2014. "The Gun Report, One Year Later", *International New York Times*, February 5.

O'Connor D. 2010. "Performance from the Outside-In", *Policing. A Journal of Policy and Practice*, 4, 152–156.

Pantazis C. and Pemberton C. 2010. "From the 'Old' to the 'New' suspect community: examining the impact of recent UK counter-terrorist legislation", *British Journal of Criminology*, 49(5), 646–666.

Peach C. 2006. "Social Integration and Social Mobility: Spatial Segregation, Intermarriage of the Caribbean Population in Britain", in G.C. Loury, T. Modood and S.M. Tezles (eds) *Ethnicity, Social Mobility, and Public Policy*, Cambridge, Cambridge University Press, 173–203.

Pew Research Center. 2006. *The Great Divide How Westerners and Muslims View Each Other*, Washington DC, Pew Global Attitude Project, June.

Pew Research Poll. 2012. Quoted by Cole D. 2012. "The American Romance with Guns", *The New York Review of Books*, September 27, 48.

Plein droit, No. 81, 2/2009. "La police et les étrangers".

Poli A. 2001. "Les jeunes face au racisme dans les quartier populaires", in M. Wieviorka and J. Ohanna (eds) *La différence culturelle*, Paris, Balland, 198–205.

Power A. and Tunstall R. 1997. *Dangerous Disorder: Riots and Violent Distrubances in Thirteen Areas of Britain, 1991–92*, New York: York Joseph Rowtree Foundation.

Reiner, R. 1985. *The Politics of the Police*, Brighton, Wheatsheaf.

Rittel H. and Webber M. 1973. "Dilemmas in a General Theory of Planning", *Policy Sciences*, 4, 155–169.

Rose R. 1982. *The Territorial Dimension in Government: Understanding the United Kingdom*, Chatham, NJ, Chatham House.

Rowe M. (ed.) 2007. *Policing Beyond MacPherson*, Cullompron, Willan.

Sabbagh D. 2003. "Judicial Uses of Subterfuge: Affirmative Action Reconsidered", *Political Science Quaterly*, 411–436.

DOI: 10.1057/9781137428004.0008

Sassen S. 2014. *Expulsions. Brutality and Complexity in the Global Economy*, Cambridge, Belknap/Harvard.

Sayad A. 1985. "Les trois âges de l'immigration", *Actes de la recherche en Sciences Sociales*, No. 5.

Scarman Lord and Justice. 1985. *The Brixton Disorders 10th–12th April, 1981*, London, HMSO.

Schain M. 2012. *The Politics of Immigration in France, Britain and the United States*, New York, Palgrave Macmillan, 2008 and 2nd print 2012.

Schnapper D. 1995. *La communauté des citoyens*, Paris, Gallimard.

Schneider C. 2014. *Police Power and Race Relations:Urban Unrest in Paris and New York. Philadelphia*, University of Pennsylvania Press.

Scott A. 1990. *Domination and the Arts of Resistance: Hidden Transcripts*, New Haven, Yale University Press.

Sherman L. 1995. "Hot Spots of Crime and Criminal Careers of Places", in J. Eck and D. Weisburg (eds) *Crime and Place*, Monsey, NY, Criminal Justice Press.

Sherman L. and Neyroud P. 2012. *Offender-Desistance Policing and the Sword of Damocles*, London, Civitas Report.

Sherman L. and Weisburg D. 1995. "General Deterrent Effects of Police Patrol in Crime Hot Spots: A Randomized Controlled Trial", *Justice Quarterly*, 12, 625–648.

Simon J. 2007. *Governing Through Crime*, Oxford, Oxford University Press.

Singh D., Rabbatts H., Marcus S. and Baroness Sherlock M. 2012. After the Riots: The Final report on the Riots, Communities and Victims Panel http://riotspanel.independent.gov.uk/wpcontent/uploads/2012/03/Riots-Panel-Final-Report1.pdf. Accessed March 29, 2012.

Skogan W. 1997. *Contacts between Police and Public: Findings from the 1992 British Crime Survey*. Home Office Research Study 134. London, HMSO.

Skogan W. (ed.) 2004. *Community Policing: Can It Work?*, Toronto, Thomson Wadsworth.

Skogan W. and Hartnett S. 1997 *Community Policing, Chicago Style*, New York, Oxford University Press.

Skolnick J. 1998. "The Colour of Law", *The American Prospect*, 39, July.

Smith D. 1987. "Policing and Urban Unrest", in J. Benyon, J. Solomos (eds) *The Roots of Urban Unrest*, Oxford, Pergamon Press, 69–74.

Smith D. 1994. "Race, Crime and Criminal Justice", in M. Maguire, R. Morgan and R. Reiner (eds) *The Oxford Handbook of Criminology*, Oxford, Clarendon Press.

DOI: 10.1057/9781137428004.0008

Smith J. 2014. "Black Town, White Power", *International New York Times*, August 19.

Stafford Smith C. 2014. "Two Nations Related by Fear", *International New York Times, April 14, 7.*

Stearns P. 2006. *American Fears. The Causes and Consequences of High Anxiety*, New York, Routledge.

Taguieff P.-A. (ed.) 1988. *La force du préjugé. Essai sur le racisme et ses doubles*, Paris, La Découverte.

Taguieff P.-A. (ed.) 2012. *Dictionnaire historique et critique du racisme*, Paris, Presses Universitaires de France.

Thuot T. 2013. Rapport au Premier Ministre *Pour une société inclusive*, February 1, 2013.

Tocqueville, A. de. 1830/1961. *De la démocratie en Amérique*, Paris, Gallimard.

Tonry M. 1995. *Malign Neglect. Race, Class and Punishment in America*, New York, Oxford University Press

Tonry M. 2008. "Preface", in T. Tyler (ed.) *Legitimacy and the Criminal Justice System*, New York, Russell Sage Foundation.

Tyler T. 1990. *Why People Obey the Law*, New Haven, Yale University Press.

Tyler T. 2004. "Enhancing Police Legitimacy", *The Annals of the American Academy of Political and Social Science*, 593, 84–99.

Waddington D., Jobard F. and King M. 2009. *Rioting in the UK and France*, Cullompron, Willan.

Waddington P. J. 1999. "Police (Canteen) Subculture. an Appreciation", *British Journal of Criminology*, 39(2), 237–309.

Waddington P. J. 2009. "Search", in A. Wakefield and J. Fleming (eds) *The Sage Dictionary of Policing*, London, Sage, 281–283.

Waddington P. J. and Wright M. 2008. Police Use of Force, Firearms and Riot-Control. In T. Newburn (ed.) *Handbook of Policing*, 2nd print, Cullompton, Willan, 465–492.

Waters M. 2014. "Defining Difference: The Role of Immigrant Generation and Race in American and British Immigration Studies", *Ethnic and Racial Studies*, 37(1), 10–26.

Weber M. 1958. *The Protestant Ethic and the Spirit of Capitalism*, New York, Scribner.

Weber M. 1991. In G. Roth and C. Wittich (eds) *1922/1968 Economy and Society*, Berkeley, CA: University of California Press.

Webster C. 2007. *Understanding Race and Crime,* London, McGraw Hill.

Weil P. 2004. *Qu'est-ce qu'un Français?*, Paris, Gallimard.

DOI: 10.1057/9781137428004.0008

Westmarland L. 2010. "Dodgy customers? Can the police ever trust the public?", *Policing. A Journal of Policy and Practice*, 4(3), 291–297.

Whitman J. 2003. *Harsh Justice*, Oxford, Oxford University Press.

Wieviorka M. 2008. *La diversité*, Paris, Robert Laffont.

Wieviorka M. and Bataille P. 1992. *La France raciste*, Paris, La Découverte.

Wihtol de Wenden C. 1988. *Les immigrés et la politique. Cent-cinquante ans d'évolution*, Paris, Presses de Sciences-Po.

Wihtol de Wenden C. 2005. La "Seconde Génération", in R. Leveau and K. Mohsen, *Musulmans de France et d'Europe*, Paris, CNRS Editions.

Wihtol de Wenden C. 2012. *Atlas des Migrations*, Paris, Autrement, 3rd edition.

Wihtol de Wenden C. and Leveau R. 2007. *La beurgeoisie,* Paris, CNRS Editions.

Wilson W. J. 1987. *The Truly Disadvantaged*, Chicago, Chicago University Press.

Wilson J. Q. and Kelling G. 1982. "Broken Windows: The Police and Neighborhood Safety", *Atlantic Monthly,* March, 29–38.

Zadgrodzki M. 2014. Interview, Focus Program, France 4 TV, May 16.

Zauberman R. and Levy R. 2003. "The French State, the Police and Minorities", *Criminology,* 41, 4, 1065–1100.

Zolberg A. 2006. *A Nation by Design*, Cambridge, MA, Harvard University Press.

Zsolt N. 2007. *Muslims in Europe: Berlin, London, Paris. Bridges and Gaps in Public Opinion*, Princeton, NJ, Gallup World Poll.

DOI: 10.1057/9781137428004.0008

Index

DOI: 10.1057/9781137428004.0009

DOI: 10.1057/9781137428004.0009

DOI: 10.1057/9781137428004.0009

DOI: 10.1057/9781137428004.0009

DOI: 10.1057/9781137428004.0009

DOI: 10.1057/9781137428004.0009

Lightning Source UK Ltd.
Milton Keynes UK
UKOW04n1552221215

265233UK00003B/40/P